The Clinical Directorate

Edited b

Noel Au

Operatio
The Opu

Sue Do

Fellow in
Templeto

Forewo

Christo

Medical
Board D

HS Trust

Surrey KT18 7EG

Rad
Oxf

©1997 Noel Austin and Sue Dopson

Radcliffe Medical Press Ltd
18 Marcham Road, Abingdon, Oxon OX14 1AA, UK

Radcliffe Medical Press, Inc.
141 Fifth Avenue, New York, NY 10010, USA

British Library Cataloguing in Publication Data

A catalogue record for this book is available from the British Library.

ISBN 1 85775 037 3

Library of Congress Cataloging-in-Publication Data is available.

Typeset by Marksbury Multimedia Ltd
Printed and bound by Biddles Ltd, Guildford and King's Lynn

Contents

Foreword

Most of us prefer the things around us – transport, education, supermarkets etc. – to work effectively, efficiently and courteously: in other words to be *well-managed*. Modern hospitals are amongst the most complex of organizations, and it is in some ways quite extraordinary that the concept of managing a hospital is so new (and in some quarters so reviled). Like medicine, modern management theory and practice has come a long way and comprises a set of skills and concepts that need to be mastered for management to be effective.

Few would disagree that hospital consultants generally excel at managing their patients. Most (though sadly not all) are also pretty well-organized individuals, and many lead and inspire excellent clinical teams. It is therefore hardly surprising that many consultants underestimate how difficult management can be: until they try it themselves. Clinicians increasingly have a significant role to play in managing their services, staff and budgets, and also in ensuring the long term success of their organization.

Most UK hospitals now operate some kind of clinical management structure, usually based on 'clinical directorates', and clinical staff may be asked to take on the role of clinical director or manager. Few will be well-prepared for this and many will come to appreciate the complexities, challenges and rewards of management the hard way.

This excellent book will go a long way towards helping clinicians to grasp the important concepts and language of management, particularly as it relates to their clinical directorate and hospital environment. It focuses specifically on the human relationships and interactions that underpin effective clinical teams facing the challenge of change – as well as covering the more technical aspects such as finance, information and planning. It is written in a clear and concise style by a team of experts who have long experience in management training for doctors and other health care professionals. It is just the sort of book I wish had been available when I first became involved in management nearly a decade ago.

Christopher Bunch
Medical Director, Oxford Radcliffe Hospital NHS Trust
Board Director, British Association of Medical Managers

October 1996

List of contributors

Noel Austin, Operations Director, The OPUS Partnership, Newbury

David Bowden, Chief Executive, Merrett Health Risk Management Ltd

Professor Christopher J Cowton, University Business School, Huddersfield

Dr Sue Dopson, Fellow in Organizational Behaviour, Templeton College, Oxford

Sid Jennings, Industrial Liaison Fellow, Templeton College, Oxford

Dr Ian Kessler, Fellow in Human Resource Management, Templeton College, Oxford

Annabelle Mark, Senior Lecturer, Middlesex University and Research Associate, Oxford Health Care Management Institute, Templeton College, Oxford

Introduction

Management is the one disease I did not think existed.

(Consultant paediatrician)

As the quotation above suggests, becoming involved in management can come as somewhat of a surprise to some senior doctors. Yet in the market-led NHS, inevitably doctors will increasingly be involved in managing. More and more consultants will be required to take on a clinical director rôle or some equivalent. Middle grade staff will face questions about management issues in their interviews for consultant posts and may themselves be drawn into a variety of managerial activities. Many medical schools are currently considering if, and to what extent, they will offer elements of management education as part of a medical degree. A telling indicator of the increased involvement of doctors in management activities has been the explosion of management training and development offerings targeted towards doctors. There is a bewildering set of choices that many Trusts find difficult to afford, now that national sources of monies for such activities have dried up. This book offers to doctors at all levels an introduction to management, grounded in the contributors' experiences of working with doctors in management. For those in search of a theoretical introduction there is already a range of accessible introductory texts on the foundations of management theory.[1,2]

We hope that after reading the book, you will:

- have a better understanding of some of the management jargon that you undoubtedly have heard used locally

- obtain a better appreciation of the managerial context in which you work

- make progress in a number of your more managerial tasks by drawing on insights, models, and frameworks offered in each chapter

- be in a better position to decide if you need to explore an area in more depth either by reading, talking to others, or undertaking some formal management training.

The contributors have written each chapter with the busy clinician in mind. The emphasis is on offering you a practical way forward in coping with the various management tasks you face.

Some readers may dip into this book to read about specific topics; others may read it from cover to cover. For the benefit of the latter category, this book is organized along the following lines.

Chapter 1: Working in teams. This may seem a surprising choice for Chapter 1 but it derives from the observation that the successful clinical director achieves that success by managing through his or her directorate management team rather than alone. In other words, members of the management team work together to carry out many management tasks. Hence an understanding of how to run a team is a necessary prerequisite to the exercise of other management skills.

Chapter 2: Managing people. In every directorate people are the most valuable resource and, with the possible exception of imaging, the most costly. Further-more, the achievement of the directorate's strategies and plans is dependent on the cooperation and support of the professionals and support staff who work in it.

Chapter 3: Negotiating. The directorate management team must negotiate with other directorates, with supplier departments, with Trust managers and, increas-ingly, directly with commissioners. Negotiating skills are therefore relevant to both developing and implementing strategic and service delivery plans.

Chapter 4: Managing change. It is often argued that managers exist primarily to manage change, since without change there is stagnation, and a stagnant organization eventually dies. An understanding of the issues surrounding change, and ways of dealing with them, is a helpful introduction to planning and implementation.

Chapter 5: Strategic planning. If management is about change, then planning for change is a key activity, and this chapter provides the tools and techniques to enable the directorate management team to develop and communicate its strategic plans.

Chapter 6: Service delivery planning. A characteristic of the health service is that every client is different, and planning service delivery is complex and difficult. However, it is possible to plan in such a messy environment, and this chapter provides an approach based on experience of planning service delivery drawn from a variety of environments.

Chapter 7: Managing financially. Finance is a way of reducing to a common denominator information about a wide range of activities and resources so that they can be compared and monitored.

Chapter 8: Information. Information systems are increasingly able to provide a wide range of information to enable the directorate team to monitor and manage service delivery and the use of all the resources at its disposal.

Chapter 9: Quality. In many ways, all the previous chapters of this book are focused on one objective – the planning and delivery of quality care. This chapter considers what additional insights we can gain from the tools and techniques developed by the quality 'industry'.

We have chosen these areas for elaboration because they are issues that doctors have described to us as key aspects of their managerial work. Before launching into chapters a necessary first step, it seems to us, is to spend a little time considering the overall organizational context in which you work, as it is this context that significantly influences managing in the NHS. To this end, the rest of the introduction considers the current pressures on the NHS as an organization and the structural arrangements in place to deal with these. It also discusses developments designed to improve the involvement of doctors in management.

Working in a complex environment

If we stand back from our day-to-day work and attempt to take an overview of the health service, its first and most striking feature is its complexity. In a very short space of some 60 or 70 years, modern scientific medicine has rapidly developed sophisticated levels of knowledge and technology which are applied to an ever-expanding range of health problems. It is the complexity of modern health care which poses such a diverse challenge to everyone involved in the management of health services. A second feature of modern health care is the pace of change. The developments in new treatments, services, and skills within the health service mean that, for much of the time, people working in the health service are concerned with the management of change. Figure 1 shows a simple model of how the health service works.[3] We can use this model to identify some of the sources and complexities in health care.

The changing demands faced by the health service take many forms:

● the health problems presented by patients

● changes in demography

● technology and public opinion.

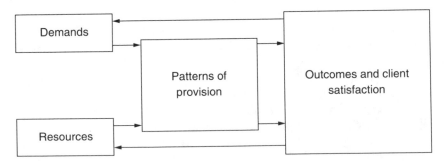

Figure 1: A simple model of the key components of a health care system.

The resources involved in the provision of health services are changing. The pattern of finance in the health service since the introduction of the internal market is much more complex. The patterns of provision of health care are also changing; in particular, changes can be seen in treatments and services provided to patients, and the ways in which the services are structured and organized. There is also increased emphasis on measuring outcomes. This provides feedback on the basis of which modifications may be made to the first three elements of the model – demands, resources, and patterns of provision. This complexity has always been a feature of the NHS and doctors clearly have an influence on each of these aspects. Hence successive reorganizations of the NHS have sought, in a variety of ways, to involve doctors in management. The next section briefly reviews these.

Attempts to involve doctors in management

The 1974 reorganization of the NHS was the first significant attempt. A consultant and GP representative, along with an administrator, nurse, treasurer, and medical officer, worked as a consensus management team charged with managing health services at the various levels of the NHS.

Researchers looking at the impact of consensus management teams on local health systems have noted a marked contrast between doctors' involvement on the national and local stage. Nationally doctors have taken a lead in securing a position of influence in both the formation of the NHS and subsequent reorganizations in 1974 and 1982. However on the local stage, there appears to be a great reluctance on the part of doctors to get involved in the local management of health services. Representatives of the profession working in consensus management teams at this time seem unwilling to give time to the demands of the representative rôle; they feel vulnerable when taking decisions because of the lack of information and for fear of offending their colleagues. In part, the reluctance of doctors to be involved in managing local health care delivery can be explained by the over-complicated medical advisory machinery created in 1974. However, the most significant reason suggested by available studies is that doctors exercise great influence on the patterns and priorities of health care without needing to take up formerly defined administrative rôles.

The next significant reorganization of the NHS was that of the introduction of general management in 1983. This reorganization dispensed with the system of consensus management and replaced it with a general manager from any discipline managing a team of people that included a representative of the medical profession. Griffiths saw general managers as the linchpin of dynamic management.[4] He cast them as chief executives, providing leadership and capitalizing on existing high levels of dedication and expertise amongst NHS staff of all disciplines. In addition, he expected general managers to stimulate 'initiative, urgency, and vitality' amongst staff, to bring about a constant search for major change in cost improvement, to motivate staff, and ensure that professional functions were effectively fed into the general management process.

Implicit in the report are two important assumptions about doctors. Firstly, that the development of budgets at unit level would lead to closer involvement of clinicians in managing resources and allow workload service objectives to be related to financial and manpower allocations. Secondly, that members of the medical profession would become general managers. The Griffiths Report represented a distinctly different approach to managing medical power and reflected a more critical attitude towards the power of doctors to shape patterns of care. This more aggressive stance by the government was fuelled by many complex factors, most prominent of which was the need to rein in public expenditure.

In practice, only a few general managers came from a medical background and there has been a subsequent decline in numbers; management budgeting has met with variable results.[5] In short, the consensus of the available commentaries has been that professionals playing a key rôle have been slow to embrace the cultural change from the administration to the management of the health service.

Since the publication of the 1989 White Paper outlining the latest reorganization of the NHS based on the internal market model, there has been a significant increase in activity targeted towards involving doctors in management. It is worth spending a little time considering the current structure of the NHS (Figure 2). This is the context in which you now work but our experience of working with doctors has been that very rarely do they have the time, or in some cases the inclination, to fathom how this structure works.

Chris Ham has produced a helpful overview of the new structure following the publication of the White Paper;[6] the most significant elements include:

- the separation of purchaser and provider rôle
- the creation of self-governing NHS Trusts
- the transformation of district health authorities into purchasers of service
- the introduction of GP fundholding
- the use of contracts or service agreements to provide links between purchaser and providers
- the slimming down and reorganization of Regions and the Department of Health.

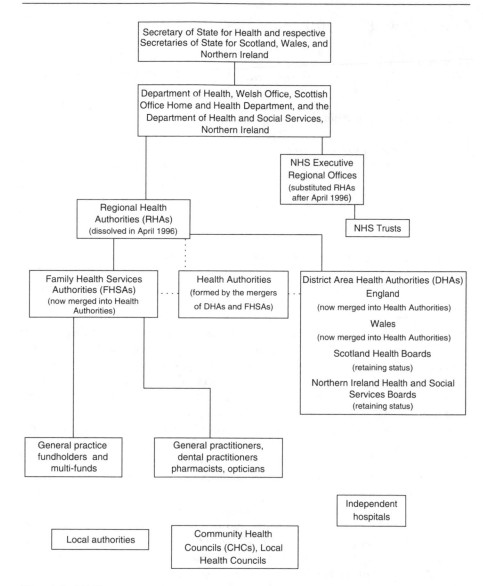

Figure 2: NHS structure.

Specific strategies for managing clinical activity

Hunter helpfully outlines three, following the White Paper changes, along a continuum of minimal to maximal involvement by external agencies (Box 1).[7]

Box 1: Managing clinical activity in the NHS

Raising professional standards	Medical audit Standards and guidelines Accreditation
Involving doctors in management	Budgets for doctors Resource management initiative Doctor managers
External management control of doctors	Managing medical work Changing doctors' contracts Extending provider competition

---

The first strategy focuses on encouraging self-help in doctors to raise professional standards by medical audit and the use of standards and guidelines. The second relies on involving doctors in management by delegating budgetary responsibility to doctors and appointing doctors as managers. The final strategy rests on an attempt to buttress external management control by changing doctors' contracts and encouraging managers to supervise medical work more closely.

Policy makers and senior managers in the NHS have concentrated on the second of these strategies in their efforts to manage clinical activity. The strategy of involving professionals in managerial work is common to a range of organizations in both public and private sectors. For example: the resource management initiative, which replaced early experiments of management budgeting but which is similarly intended to bring doctors into management, has been rolled out of the 12 hospital and community pilot sites to traditional sites.[7] In most hospitals in the NHS, clinical directorates have been set up to manage a budget. Consultants have been encouraged to take on the job of clinical director, often supported by a business manager and a nurse manager. They have considerable responsibilities covering issues such as outpatient scheduling, inpatient admissions, quality assurance, customer relations, and medical nursing resources.

As any 'doctor manager' will tell you, it is a tough job. It is useful to consider the experiences of some of the doctors we have worked with – mainly consultants – who have moved into management rôles, and what they tell us about the difficulties of such a move.

Often consultants who have taken on clinical director rôles note that their job descriptions do not reflect what they feel is the core of their management job, the task of influencing their colleagues to think about the future development of the service in the context of limited resources and a more competitive environment. Fitzgerald has also noted that although clinical managers often define their own rôles in terms of high levels of change management, the job descriptions of clinical directors in her sample focused on the conventional managerial tasks of staff management, team management, representation, and setting and monitoring performance standards.[8]

Why do consultants get involved in management?

Several factors are often cited aside from the purchaser/provider shake-up. The most frequently mentioned reason is the fear of being managed. As one put it: 'I am not having somebody who isn't a consultant telling me what to do about my service'. Boredom is yet another commonly given reason: 'One of the drawbacks of being a consultant is that you get the job and that is it for 25 years. Faced with this, management becomes an attractive option'.

All consultants we have worked with are very interested in seeing how management can improve their service. However, this more 'positive' reason has to be balanced by the fact that the majority are reluctant to enter management, do so for one or more of the reasons discussed above, or because it is a case of 'Buggin's turn'.

Concerns about becoming involved in management

These typically centre around resources and relationships. Very often doctors have a managerial workload that far exceeds the 'official' time allocated to it. This naturally has an impact on clinical work, teaching, and keeping up with developments in their speciality. A fear of alienating colleagues and undermining clinical relationships because of an involvement in management, is also a common concern.

> A three year reign as clinical director does not offer enough security to take the necessary risks that might influence professional colleagues' behaviour in any significant way.

Many doctors feel guilty about placing extra work on to overworked colleagues. The absence of a career path for doctors going into management also acts as a constraint on the time and effort spent engaging in work doctors term managing. The quotation below reflects another major concern about becoming involved in management:

> The majority of consultants view the NHS as under-resourced and under-valued by the present political masters, and therefore feel it is not a good time to get involved

in management.... Management is currently seen as having to live within resources that are totally inadequate for health needs.

The low status of management in the NHS was given as a factor inhibiting doctors' involvement in management. As one consultant noted: 'The prevalent attitude amongst consultants is that any fool can do management. They think it is all commonsense. They think it is easy compared to the serious business of medicine'.

How can we begin to explain the seeming reluctance of doctors to respond to the various attempts to increase their involvement in management? Most commentators cite the very different training and education each group receives. General managers, for example, tend to stress the virtues of inter-personal skills and of enlisting the cooperation of others. They expect to subsume individual interests to those of the organization. They are trained to be aware of the wider implications of any activity within the organization. They also expect to make optimal use of limited resources and are used to working towards long-term goals. Doctors, in contrast, expect to strive for the best available evidence before making a decision. They are used to working to short-term operational goals. Furthermore, doctors are hardened by a career progression which makes tough physical and emotional demands on them and tends to limit their social contacts to people working in the hospital. They rarely receive any training in management or organizational skills until they are quite senior. There is, therefore, a fundamental conflict of interests, yet often government, general managers, doctors, and health service commentators seem to regard the conflict between managers and doctors as simply a conflict on the level of ideas about the relative merits or demerits of management.

There is also an explanation referred to earlier, namely that doctors do not need to become involved in management because they are significantly able to shape the way in which health services are managed without taking up formal rôles.

References

1 Grint K. (1995) *Management – A sociological introduction.* Sage.
2 Anthony PD. (1986) *The Foundations of Management.* Tavistock.
3 Dopson S and Fitzpatrick R. (1990) *The manager and the wider world. Book 10, The Effective Manager Course.* The Open University.
4 Griffiths R. (1983) *DHSS, NHS, Management inquiry.* DHSS, London.
5 Harrison S, Hunter D, Marnoch G *et al.* (1993) *Just managing: power and culture in the NHS.* Macmillan Press.
6 Ham CJ. (1994) *Management and competition in the new NHS.* Radcliffe Medical Press.

7 Hunter DJ. (1991) Managing medicine: a response to the crisis. *Social Science and Medicine.* **32**(4): 44–449.

8 Fitzgerald L. (1993) *Clinicians in to management: the agenda for change and training.* Paper prepared for Professions and Management Conference, University of Stirling, August.

Working in teams

Annabelle Mark

> I hear and I forget
> I see and I remember
> I do and I understand.
>
> Chinese proverb

Much of medical education and management education share the principles upon which this proverb is based, and common to both is a need to understand working in teams. This will not come from reading this chapter or watching how teams work but from active participation in the process of management in clinical and management teams in community and hospital trusts.

Developing teams

All doctors are familiar with the idea of working in teams, and participation in teams is part of the training process to develop clinical and interpersonal skills relevant to the doctor's rôle and patients' needs. Joining and leaving such teams is also a familiar pattern of activity for junior doctors during training. One of the lessons learned from this is the need for adaptability and flexibility, to enable them to fit quickly into different teams and thus maximize the opportunities to develop medical skills.

Similarly in management, joining teams is not always a matter of choice, nor are the other members of the team always the people we would choose to work with. The skill is in identifying and understanding the opportunities and constraints provided by any particular team. This will also help to ensure that, if you are able to choose new team members, you can choose the right person for both the team and the job.

The familiarity with the clinical team rôle can prove to be both a help and a hindrance when it comes to operating within management teams. This is particularly true in the case of clinical directorate teams; the primary task is not the management of individual patients but the management of limited resources to meet patient needs through the contracting process.

However, managers in the reformed NHS have often used clinical teams as the starting point for the development of the clinical directorate or management structures, without giving enough thought to what they need to do to change these teams to make them effective managerially as well as clinically. Differentiating the rôles can only happen if a better understanding of team working is available to all participants in the team process, allowing members to distinguish the managerial and clinical aspects of their rôles and tasks. To consider this issue in more depth it is necessary to look at what a team is, how it functions, and why it may fail.

What is a team?

All organizations are made up of groups of individuals working together. These groups can be formal, put together by the organization, e.g. a surgical firm; or informal, brought together by a shared interest, e.g. an interest in rugby or religion. The standard definition of a group[1] is any number of people who:

- interact with each other
- are psychologically aware of one another
- perceive themselves to be a group.

So how do groups differ from teams? Teams not only share interests but together focus on common goals and interdependencies. This means they need to understand the behaviour of participants both as individuals and as members of the group, as well as the tasks and objectives of the team.

Within the clinical team the desired objective is the delivery of effective care to patients by a group of individuals who, initially at least, have their activities determined by the professional rôle for which they have been trained. Their contribution is that of a specialist providing knowledge and skills in a specific area, understanding the detail and technicalities, but often perhaps failing to see the 'big picture'. This failure to integrate technical and specialist knowledge into the 'big picture' is the evolutionary consequence of the development of scientific knowledge, often referred to as reductionism. Furthermore, it is one of the reasons why some doctors have reverted to a more holistic approach in medicine. Within medicine the specialties of general practice, paediatrics, and geriatrics are likely to be most familiar with such integrative approaches to their work. Team working can also help to develop and establish the relationships and interdependencies between specialists for the benefit of patients, but requires changes in knowledge, skills, and attitudes if it is to really succeed. At present the patient is the point at which these different specialists meet and define the boundaries of possibility for their contributions. It is through the patient, more often than the team, that they discover these interdependencies.

However, clinicians eliminate possible concerns about the well-being of patients through another key factor that influences the way clinical teams work: the formal professional relationships that operate between the various professional groups. In management we would describe these relationships as a hierarchy. Hierarchy exists not only within professions, the opinion of a consultant taking precedence over the opinion of a registrar, but also between professions, where the opinion of a doctor will frequently override that of a nurse or one of the professions allied to medicine (Box 1.1). This hierarchy is enshrined not just in practice but, in some instances, also in law. This medical supremacy is implicit unless the doctor invades the skill areas of the other professionals. When this happens, we see boundary disputes between rôles, such as when a doctor tries to tell a nurse how to nurse. Further problems can occur when such rôles are themselves developing and changing, such as in the development of the hybrid rôle of the nurse practitioner, which crosses the professional boundaries of both the doctor and nurse rôles. Some doctors will recognize such boundary violations; others will use their status in the professional hierarchy to overrule the opinion of other professionals. Resorting to status as a method of controlling issues will affect the outcomes of the team development process by damaging the atmosphere within the team, commitment, professional participation in the task in hand, and, ultimately, the outcome for the patient.

In summary, it can be said that a successful team will develop a shared set of complementary behaviour patterns expected of the individuals within it. These rôles, which are defined by the duties, obligations, and expectations which accompany a particular position, will be based on factors such as:

- norms, or the acceptable standards shared by the group. These can be both explicit: 'how we do things around here', and implied through behaviour, e.g. always calling nurses by their first name and consultants by their surnames in front of patients

- status or prestige and ranking within the group which may be for reasons of age, profession, experience, or other cultural factors determined as relevant by the group

- cohesiveness, or the extent to which the group shares group norms, values, and goals; this is most often shown in how effective the group is seen to be by others.

Teams are formed in organizations because they usually produce more and better ideas than any one individual could. They also allow those who have the best idea of the consequences at the 'front line' to make the decisions. This enables empowerment of the groups who are given the freedom, scope, and choices to achieve organizational goals in the way they think fit. This in theory should democratize

Box 1.1: Interruptions as an indicator of hierarchy

An easy test of hierarchy and pecking orders in groups is to draw a visual representation or 'sociogram' of interactions which show interruptions; you can also indicate above each arrow how often this occurs:

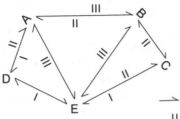

—→ = Direction of interruption

III = No of interruptions

Figure 1.1: Sociogram to establish pecking order in groups.

In the illustration the arrow's direction shows who is interrupting, so:

- B is interrupted most
- A is next
- D and C are equal
- E is interrupted least.

As people feel free to interrupt others they perceive to be lower in the hierarchy than themselves it is easy to see the order of importance. Within peer groups the results will show how a pecking order has developed. You can use such information to show how professional hierarchies relevant to clinical activity are influencing decision making. These factors, while appropriate for the clinical activity, may not be appropriate to the team when they are undertaking a management rôle as we shall see.

the organization and make people feel that their opinions, both individually and collectively, will make a difference to the control within the organization.[2]

Team behaviour

Teams become involved in the need to understand different types of behaviour as a consequence of the need to work together. We can divide these types of behaviour into those associated with the task and those associated with the interactions in the group.

Task behaviour involves such activities as proposing, giving information, seeking information, and summarizing progress. Managing the interaction process is often called 'maintenance oriented' behaviour, the purpose of which is to build and support the group as a working team and can be seen in such activities as encouraging participation, reducing tension, and giving feedback. These types of behaviour are of equal importance.

However, within groups and teams there is a third set of factors, besides the task and group maintenance factors, which influence outcomes. These are the self-oriented behaviours which individuals display to achieve their individual goals. These are a necessary part of the process for individuals of negotiating and understanding their individual value, both now and in the future, and need to be acknowledged. These self-oriented behaviours can seem rather negative. They may involve such activities as attacking the position of others, diverting issues to one's own agenda, sympathy seeking and over- or under-contributing, which can be not only indicative of timidity or ignorance but also perhaps because, in some circumstances, 'silence is the most perfect expression of scorn'.[3]

Extensive research in the management process has revealed that professional rôles within teams may be necessary but are not sufficient to successful completion of the task and continuation of the team. Success depends on an understanding that team members perform not just professional or functional rôles, but also team rôles.

The most well-known description of these team rôles were characterized by Dr Meredith Belbin in 1981 and have now been updated (Figure 1.2).[4] To the original eight rôles he has added that of the specialist, which will no doubt be where many doctors would feel their rôle lies. This, however, would miss the point of involving doctors in managing the management process. Doctors need to understand that they must find team rôles, as appropriate to their personalities as to their professional skills.

Belbin has devised a series of assessment methods to determine which of these team rôles individuals are best suited to. Many management team training programmes use the method to determine team rôles for working groups. Although such analytical approaches may not be foolproof, what is not in any doubt is that a range of behavioural rôles is required within a team to make it work effectively. The critical issue is that successful teams need to incorporate the team rôles. Although other factors, such as functional or professional rôles, usually predict team membership, it is important to learn to work with the team you have, not with the team you would like.

The Belbin research not only provides a pointer to team rôles but also shows that teams of clever people or people with similar personalities will not be as effective (Figure 1.3).[4] So it is not always necessary to have the best doctor or nurse but rather one who complements the others in the team. Nor is it advisable to have people with similar personalities, even though we have a tendency to

Rôles and descriptions – team-rôle contribution		Allowable weaknesses
	**Plant:** Creative, imaginative, unorthodox. Solves difficult problems.	Ignores details. Too preoccupied to communicate effectively.
	**Resource investigator:** Extrovert, enthusiastic, communicative. Explores opportunities, develops contacts.	Over-optimistic. Loses interest once initial enthusiasm has passed.
	**Co-ordinator:** Mature, confident, a good chairperson. Clarifies goals, promotes decision-making, delegates well.	Can be seen as manipulative. Delegates personal work.
	**Shaper:** Challenging, dynamic, thrives on pressure. Has the drive and courage to overcome obstacles.	Can provoke others. Hurts people's feelings
	**Monitor evaluator:** Sober, strategic and discerning. Sees all options, judges accurately.	Lacks drive and ability to inspire others. Overly critical.
	**Team worker:** Co-operative, mild, perceptive and diplomatic. Listens, builds, averts friction, calms the waters.	Indecisive in crunch situations. Can be easily influenced.
	**Implementer:** Disciplined, reliable, conservative and efficient. Turns ideas into practical actions.	Somewhat inflexible. Slow to respond to new possibilities.
	**Completer:** Painstaking, conscientious, anxious. Searches out errors and omissions. Delivers on time.	Inclined to worry unduly. Reluctant to delegate. Can be a nit-picker.
	**Specialist:** Single-minded, self-starting, dedicated. Provides knowledge and skills in rare supply.	Contributes on only a narrow front. Dwells on technicalities. Overlooks the 'big picture'.

Figure 1.2: Belbin team roles.

select individuals like us when we are able to choose. That tendency also helps to account for why it has taken so long for women and other marginalized groups to be appointed in both managerial and medical posts. We would all much rather appoint people like ourselves with whom we feel comfortable and safe.

Type of team	Performance characteristics
 Stable, extrovert teams	Pull well together, enjoy group work; versatile approach; use resources well but inclined to be euphoric and lazy. *Results:* good on the whole, but individually rather dependent on one another and on others.
 Anxious, extrovert teams	Dynamic; entrepreneurial; good at seizing opportunities; prone to healthy altercation; easily distracted and liable to rush off at tangents. *Results:* good in rapidly changing situations but unreliable in performance at other times.
 Stable, introvert teams	Plan well; strong in organization; but slow-moving and liable to neglect new factors in a situation. *Results:* generally indifferent.
 Anxious, introvert teams	Capable of good ideas but a tendency to be preoccupied; lacking cohesion as a team. *Results:* usually poor.

Figure 1.3: Belbin pure teams.

Understanding the limitations and opportunities inherent within professional activity, personality types, and team rôles will lead to adjustment and appreciation of others in the team, all of which helps to build team cooperation and success.

Specific team rôles do not restrict team members because, while they may have preferred rôles, these can change according to circumstances. Individuals can also fulfil more than one rôle if the team is smaller than nine; this will often be their 'back up' rôle with which they feel some affinity. Furthermore, each team member should understand his or her least favoured rôle as, if shared with others, this could give rise to a weakness in the team which would need positive development. Teams, as Belbin says, need to be structured; if a team is to be successful, team members must work as hard at team development as they do at the task.

In selecting for team membership it is also useful to remember the difference between eligibility and suitability (Box 1.2).

Box 1.2: Eligibility and suitability for team membership

Eligibility   depends on considering   past achievements
Suitability   depends on predicting   future performance

Belbin suggests that we should consider both factors, with the following consequences (Table 1.1).

Table 1.1: Team membership using eligibility and suitability

		Suitability	
		+	−
Eligibility	+	Ideal fit Short stayer	Poor fit Personality
	−	Surprise fit Long stayer	Total misfit Fails both

Building groups into teams requires effort, it will not just happen because people focus on a shared task, although this can help. First we need to understand the *barriers* that exist between group members. Some of these will be stereotypes, already mentioned, which can be of a positive or negative nature. These are known as the halo and horn effects, which we adopt in our perception of others. For example, if all your previous experiences have been good when dealing with female managers you may well choose to appoint a female as opposed to a male business manager (the halo effect). Conversely, if you have only two male applicants for your vacant nursing post but your experience of male nurses has been bad, you may re-advertise the post on the grounds of lack of applicants, although it is really your perception that is the problem (the horn effect) (Box 1.3).

More sophisticated team-building activities involve weekends away and outdoor team development programmes, but also less formal activities like social events to develop team cohesiveness.

Box 1.3: Understanding each others' prejudices

A simple exercise to understand these prejudices is to get each member of the team to focus on what they think managers are like. Then ask them to describe the other professional rôles, such as nurses and doctors, in the group. The group can then share this information and see not only how they see others but also how others see them. Try to be honest.

To summarize, team building will involve setting shared goals, sharing understanding of each others' rôles and personalities, and an understanding of the team process itself. Team building requires high interaction to build trust and openness.

Team process

Developing teams requires a variety of activities described as team building. These activities will help teams to get started but will only have lasting value if they are part of a continuing team process. Teams will only really be able to understand the importance of these activities once confronted with the tasks that they are required to perform. Many studies of team process have shown a pattern of development that can provide insight and knowledge for those undergoing development. Some of these stages can be uncomfortable, but confronting these hurdles is the only way to succeed and anyway, learning cannot always be an easy or comfortable experience.

Turning to the process of the team as a whole rather than the individuals within it, considerable work has been done on the stages of team development. This includes what to look for, how to recognize the stages, where the problems may occur, and finally what happens if this process is suppressed or diverted. The most frequently used model to describe this aspect of team development is that devised by Tuckman, not least because it has a very memorable set of stages (Table 1.2).

As can be seen from the process described there are several points of possible failure in the team development process. Maturity, however, occurs not just as a factor of time and development through process but is also subject to other constraints: such as:

- team membership: size, compatibility, permanence
- work environment: task setting, communications, technology
- organization: management and leadership, culture and procedures, external pressure including threat and opportunity.

Table 1.2: Stages in group development

Forming	The testing phase where behaviour is polite guarded and watchful	Information gathering
Storming	Infighting where behaviour involves confrontation, managing conflict, opting out, de-motivation, and feeling stuck	Barrier recognition
Norming	Getting organized, developing skills to overcome barriers, giving feedback, focusing on task	Developing shared interdependence
Performing	Closeness, resourceful, flexible, supportive, tolerant	Group maturity and task progress
Adjourning	Task accomplishment, group satisfaction	Team effectiveness

Tuckman's team development wheel, as it was originally known, implies that the process of forming, storming, norming, and performing is a rolling one that can be recycled at any time. Factors that may predict such recycling of the process are:

• changes to team membership

• changes to task

• changes to environment

• changes to team norms or rôles.

Any of these changes can create conflict within the team particularly at the storming stage. This conflict can be positive or negative in outcome but should not be avoided, except in circumstances that require such temporary strategies. Avoidance should only occur temporarily if the task demands immediate action, otherwise it may damage the trust and effectiveness of the team process in the longer term. Conflict over ideas should enhance team development and indicates effective team development while conflict between personalities can have more negative outcomes leading to ineffectiveness.

Managing conflict

Conflict occurs at a number of levels and in a variety of ways. Charles Handy suggests that all conflict can be attributed to either disputes about objectives and ideologies or territories.[5] Given the development of professional rôles within health care such analysis proves very useful as a starting point for understanding conflict within teams.

Conflict in objectives and ideologies can occur because doctors may have as their primary motivation scientific research while nurses are concerned with the care of the patient. Territorial conflict can be seen, for example, in the way that doctors for a long time resisted the introduction of the nurse practitioner rôle because it violated the territorial boundaries that differentiated them from nursing. Many managers now find that the rôle of doctors as managers is violating the boundaries of the managerial rôle. This has implications for the successful continuation of the operation of management teams in the NHS through clinical directorates or their equivalent. However the difference between negative and positive conflict can only be determined by the effect that it has on outcome, as demonstrated by the successful fulfilment of the team's tasks and objectives. So, for example, disputes over who does what which are discussed, confronted, and resolved in a team will lead to greater rôle clarity. This is agreeing and understanding exactly who should be doing what and thus enabling the team to proceed more competently with the task in hand.

Conflict can arise between individuals both within groups and between groups. Conflict in this sense implies perceived incompatible differences. Society has always viewed conflict as something that should be avoided; there is much evidence to support this view in our daily lives and individual behaviours. However this traditional view has been replaced by a developing understanding of the value of conflict in causing change and growth to individuals, groups, and organizations.[6] This has developed for a number of reasons, but in team terms arises in part from an examination of why some teams or groups have failed even though they have displayed shared goals and interdependencies. One example of team failure has been described as groupthink,[7] in which the group becomes more important than the tasks it has to perform. This leads to a range of behaviours which can have disastrous results, such as:

- a sense of invulnerability within the group

- unquestioned belief in the morality of the group

- pressure on group members to conform suppressing minority or unpopular ideas; members who oppose this are ostracized

- rationalization of the unacceptable to achieve consensus in spite of warning signs

- maintaining an illusion of unanimity

- self censorship of any deviation from group norms and consensus.

In these circumstances several approaches to the problem may be required, ultimately including possible dispersal of the team, but it will often require an external review of the situation before anything can be done.

Another phenomenon that some researchers suggest is a function of group behaviour is a willingness to take greater risks than any one individual would be willing to on his or her own. The reality of this assumption is not altogether convincing as much of it is based on experimental research. An alternative view is that a group is just as likely to function on the basis that its members 'individually can do nothing but as a group decide that nothing can be done';[8] this leads to stagnation and ineffectiveness.

Whether conflict has arisen as part of the process or has been generated to transcend present problems within the team, it has to be managed appropriately.[6] Strategies for managing conflict are:

- allow it to run its course
- prevent further dispute by separation or diversion
- contain it by setting limits
- reduce it by negotiation.

Not suppressing conflict but encouraging it may seem to be a recipe for chaos but like that theory's scientific roots it does not mean utter confusion, or explosive instability but rather 'It is constrained instability; a combination of order and disorder in which patterns of behaviour continually unfold in unpredictable but similar, familiar, yet irregular forms'.[9] Not managing the conflict may be the most creative response of all but, as with chaos theory, we cannot predict the ultimate pattern that develops. Intervention may also be required to actively resolve the situation, even when it has been purposefully generated, because of time constraints or other external pressures. Strategies for resolving conflict range from:

- confrontation
- focusing on superordinate goals and shared aims
- expansion of resources
- smoothing or playing down differences
- compromise
- neglect.

All these strategies can be undertaken and may require various approaches through:

- *negotiation:* where the two parties meet
- *mediation:* where a third party effects communication
- *arbitration:* where a third party has binding powers to resolve the dispute on behalf of all parties involved.

In teams it is likely that negotiation, perhaps in the context of the rest of the group who could act as mediators or arbitrators, will be the most appropriate option. In mature and effective groups:

- conflict is task based and does not centre on socio–emotional issues
- differences are accepted and group conformity is not an objective

- decisions are not forced, and come about through rational discussion
- group processes and interactions are known by the members of the group.

Determining group effectiveness can be difficult but there are warning signs of ineffectiveness which are summarized by MacGregor in Table 1.3[10] and bring many of the issues already discussed together.

Table 1.3: Contrasting behaviours in effective and ineffective groups

Effective groups	Ineffective groups
1 Group atmosphere is informal, comfortable, relaxed; no obvious tensions; no boredom; a working atmosphere of people who are both involved and interested.	1 The atmosphere reflects indifference, boredom or tension. The group is not challenged by its task or genuinely involved in it.
2 Lot of discussion which is task relevant and in which everyone participates.	2 A few people dominate the discussion and contributions are frequently off the point with no attempts made to keep the group on track.
3 The task or objective of the group is well understood; it has been arrived at through discussion and all members are committed to it.	3 From what is said, it is difficult to understand what the group task or objective is; people have different, private objectives which they are attempting to achieve in the group; there is no common objective.
4 People listen to each other and ideas are freely expressed.	
5 Disagreement is expressed not suppressed or overriden by premature group action, those who disagree do so genuinely and expect to be heard.	4 People do not really listen to each other and ideas are ignored or overridden; people leave such meetings having failed to express their ideas and feelings, being afraid of ridicule or undue criticism.
6 Decisions are reached by consensus, but the group does not allow apparent consensus to mask real disagreement, formal voting is minimized, as it tends to be divisive; the group does not accept a simple majority as a proper basis for action.	5 Disagreements are generally not dealt with effectively; they may be suppressed for fear of open conflict; where they are not suppressed, there may be 'open warfare' of one faction attempting to dominate another; there may be 'tyranny of the minority' in which an individual or sub-group is so aggressive that the majority accedes to his or its wishes in in order to preserve the peace or get on with the task.
7 Constructive criticism occurs and is not of a personal kind.	
8 People are free to express their personal feelings as well as their ideas.	
9 When action is taken, clear assignments are made and accepted.	
10 The chairperson does not dominate discussion, rather leadership shifts depending upon the issue under discussion.	6 Decisions/actions are often taken prematurely before the real issues are examined or resolved; a simple majority is considered to be sufficient, with the majority expected to go along with the decision; this creates resentment and a lack of commitment to the decision by the minority.
11 The group is self-conscious about its own operations; whether the problem is procedural or interpersonal, the group will try to resolve the problem before proceeding.	

Continued

– continued

Effective groups	Ineffective groups
12 Power struggles as such do not occur in the group; the issue is not who controls but how the job gets done.	7 Criticism creates embarrassment and tension; it is often personal and destructive. 8 People hide their feelings; they are not considered an appropriate area for discussion. 9 Responsibility for action when it is taken is unclear, and there is a lack of confidence that individuals who have been so designated will carry out their responsibility. 10 The leadership is fixed and resides in the chairperson who sits at the 'head of the table'. 11 There is no discussion in the group about its own operations or maintenance functions.

What many teams require, to change from an ineffective to effective way of working, is good leadership; this does not necessarily mean one leader within the group. Leadership is about gaining confidence in the team, its task, and the special skills and information which individuals bring with them. The most well-known approach to this issue in the UK is that developed by John Adair through *action-centred leadership* which seeks to increase effectiveness within the group by combining concern for task, maintenance, and individual needs.[11] The approach emphasizes the overlapping nature of these issues, the lack of match between the three factors, and the tension that this creates, which is where the leader's rôle becomes important (Figure 1.4).

The action-centred leader balances the three areas of team process while at the same time drawing on other leadership skills within the group; for this the leader must be:

- aware of group process, both overt and covert

- understanding of appropriate needs to a particular situation

- have the skill to do the above, which is judged by the group response.

The team may choose different members to undertake this leadership rôle depending on the nature of the task. While the chairman or coordinator may often take the position it may be appropriate to pass it to, for example, the shaper, plant, or monitor evaluator, especially when the task falls within their professional as well as their team rôle. This will be dependent to some extent on the style of leadership required for the task and the individuals involved. Style, which is also a focus of the action-centred approach, can be explained as a continuum from telling people what to do to asking them what they want to do (Figure 1.5).[12] It will also depend on the leader's preferences in focusing on the people or the task. Increasingly it is now apparent that taking the followers with you is a

Figure 1.4: Action-centred leadership.

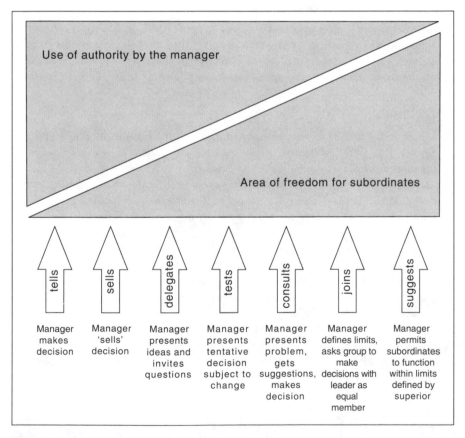

Figure 1.5: Management styles.

prerequisite for successful completion of the task, especially where the decision has long-term implications. Fast decisions at the 'tell' end of the continuum will succeed in the short term but may have negative outcomes for the leader in the longer term, whereas democratizing the decisions is likely to ensure that the team understands and owns the consequences. There is a place for the various types of leadership but it does depend on the nature of the team and task, and the types and time frames for decisions. Leaders must also have well developed influencing skills, especially when working with their peers and other professional groups.

In summary, leadership in organizations where people and decisions are likely to be around for some time, requires an appropriate approach. This should incorporate the team, task, and individual needs trio to provide an outcome that will be acceptable to everyone in both the short and, when necessary, the long term.

Summary of chapter

Management teams are important to large organizations as a way of allocating work and improving efficiency and effectiveness; they also allow everyone to participate and fully utilize their professional and personal skills to the benefit of themselves, the team, the organization, and last but not least, in health care, the patient.

References

1 Schien EH. (1988) *Organisational psychology*. 3rd Edition. Prentice Hall.
2 Semler R. (1993) *Maverick – the success story behind the world's most unusual workplace*. Arrow Business Books.
3 Shaw GB. (1921) *Back to Methusulah: a metabiological pentateuch*. Constable.
4 Belbin RM. (1993) *Team rôles at work*. Butterworth Heinemann.
5 Handy C. (1993) *Understanding organizations*. Penguin Books.
6 Pascale R. (1990) *Managing on the edge: how successful companies use conflict to stay ahead*. Penguin Books.
7 Janis I. (1982) *Victims of groupthink*. Houghton-Mifflin.
8 Allen FA. (1978) In: *Quotations for our time*. (ed) LJ Peter. Souvenir Press.
9 Stacey R. (1992) *Managing chaos – dynamic business strategies in an unpredictable world*. Kogan Page.
10 MacGregor D. (1960) *The human side of enterprise*. McGraw-Hill.
11 Adair J. (1983) *Effective leadership*. Gower Press.
12 Tannenbaum R and Schmidt W. (1958) How to choose a leadership pattern. *Harvard Business Review*. March/April.

Further reading

Markham U. (1993) *How to deal with difficult people*. Thorsons (HarperCollins imprint).

Managing people

Ian Kessler

Clinical productivity varies by up to 50 per cent between similar organizations and much of this variation results from the way that staff are organized and managed. Productivity will be maximized if staff are well informed about the organization and clear about what is expected of them personally; able to carry out their required task; motivated; and given feedback on how well they have done. If these human resource tasks are not performed well, costly problems such as job dissatisfaction, sickness absence, and staff turnover may grow.

Audit Commission (1994)[1]

Introduction

One of the most significant areas of responsibility given to Trusts on their establishment as legal bodies was that of employer. Trusts are now able to employ staff in their own right and on the basis of distinctive terms and conditions. This represents an important challenge to clinical directors for a number of reasons.

- Staff abilities and behaviours are crucial to efficient and effective service provision. 'Staff are our most important resource' has become a modern day organizational cliché, but as with any cliché it retains an enduring truth that is particularly pertinent in the health service.

- This new found responsibility as an employer represents a challenge because it constitutes such a departure from the past. Traditionally employees in the health service have managed according to centrally determined procedures and standard terms and conditions. As a consequence, local expertise and policies in these areas need to be developed.

- It is increasingly apparent that staff management issues cannot be left to the personnel specialist. The success of a clinical directorate will be based on the ability of clinical directors and their colleagues to manage their staff effectively.

- The process of developing approaches to the management of staff remains complex not least because the freedoms given are in important respects constrained by a range of external and internal factors. Trusts have to navigate their way through these constraints in developing their approaches to the management of human resources, and the decisions they make have an impact on the management of individual clinical directorates.

What is human resource management?

Human resource management has been defined by Armstrong[2] as being concerned with:

- obtaining, developing, and motivating human resources required by the organization to achieve its objectives
- developing an organization structure and climate and evolving a management style which will promote cooperation and commitment throughout the organization
- making the best use of the skills and capacities of all those employed in the organization
- ensuring that the organization meets its social and legal responsibilities towards its employees, with particular regard to the conditions of employment and quality of working life provided for them.

Within this broad definition, human resource management can be seen to comprise four key elements (Box 2.1):

Human resource approaches, philosophies, and styles

The development of an approach to the management of human resource is crucially dependent upon how such an approach is related to broader organizational strategy and structure. Figure 2.1 distinguishes between different levels of decision making within the organization. It indicates that there is a strong link between different levels of decision making. First order decisions on organization mission and purpose have a powerful influence on second order decisions related to organizational form and systems of financial control and performance monitoring. These upstream decisions in turn have a major impact on downstream human resource approaches, constraining but in so doing, defining the scope for choice in this area.

The relationship between the different levels of decision making is not, however, straightforward. As the model makes clear, third order human resource decisions can have a major impact on first order decision making. This is particularly true in the health service where not only has the treatment of staff traditionally been linked to certain public policy objectives but where, as already

Box 2.1: Elements of human resource management

Interested or involved parties	employees and their representatives managers and their representatives central government and its representatives
External and internal influences	legislative frameworks (British and European Community) technology labour markets social values and ideologies product markets trade union power policy government policy organization culture

A number of policy areas	recruitment and selection
	labour utilization
	appraisal and training and
	    development (performance
	    management)
	reward systems
	communication system

A set of outcomes	**human resource outcomes**
	strategic integration: the way in
	    which HR policies support the
	    achievement of broader business
	    strategies and are mutually
	    supportive of one another
	commitment: employee attachment to
	    their work and the organization
	flexibility: employee adaptability in
	    terms of task and skill
	quality: in terms of the staff employed
	    and the services produced
	organizational outcomes
	high job performance
	high problem solving
	low turnover
	low absence
	low grievance level

pressures/influences

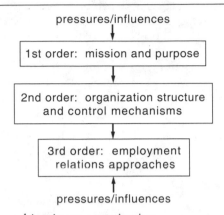

Figure 2.1: Decision making in an organization.

noted, staff often constitute the service, rendering their management crucial to the pursuit of goals such as 'service quality' and 'customer sensitivity'.

The second component of the model distinguishes between different philosophies or styles which might be chosen by the organization within the context of upstream decisions. Purcell defines management style as a 'distinctive set of guiding principles, written or otherwise, which set parameters to and signposts for management action regarding the way the employees are treated and particular events handled'.[3]

The matrix below (Figure 2.2) sets out in a modified form the management styles distinguished by Purcell and Ahlstrand. The matrix is based upon the assumption that in many organizations management style is defined by the way in which the organization treats the individual employee (individualism) *and* the

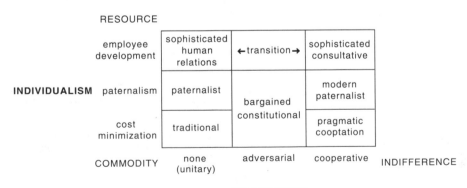

Figure 2.2: The Human Resources Management Style Matrix.

trade union or professional association (collectivism). Thus the individual may be treated as a cost to be minimized, in a paternalistic way with certain benefits given at the discretion of management, or as 'treasured' resource to be developed. The collective may be excluded (unitarist approach) or dealt with on an adversarial or cooperative manner. Given the decline in union power the organization may also decide to treat the unions with indifference. Within any organization more than one style might be adopted. For example, style may vary according to the group of employees concerned. Three of the styles appear particularly important in the health service context:

- *bargained constitutional:* most closely associated with the traditional style in the health service, underpinned by strong and adversarial unions

- *sophisticated consultation:* a style many Trusts might find attractive, combining cooperation with unions in pursuit of developmental employee goals

- *pragmatic cooptation:* based upon shared union–management interests in controlling costs and minimizing the 'pain caused' to staff by such control.

The style matrix (Figure 2.2) is useful in addressing a number of important questions.

- What is the Trust's current style?

- Does it support the Trust's mission, purpose, and structure?

- If not, is there a more appropriate style and what moves can be made in working towards it?

Defined in these terms, style can be seen as the intention and purpose underpinning management's approach to the handling of its staff. Intention and purpose are crucial in shaping the design, implementation, and operation of the procedures and techniques falling within the main human resource policy areas distinguished. Attention is given to each of these policy areas in turn, noting the scope for variation and choice available in each.

Recruitment and selection

Strike has identified the following stages (Table 2.1) when recruiting and selecting new members of staff and the time taken to complete each.[4] This process may appear lengthy and therefore frustrating but it needs to be adhered to as a means of ensuring that the following questions are satisfactorily addressed.

Table 2.1: Typical recruitment timetable

Stage	Time (days)
Conduct exit interview	1
Review the post	5
Prepare the job description	1
Prepare personnel specification	1
Prepare and place advertisement	8
Closing date	7
Short listing for interview	4
Interview notification	7
Pre-employment checks	7
Offer of employment	2
Notice period potentially required	30
Total process	73

Is there a vacancy and how should it be filled?

When a vacancy arises the first response should be to review the post to establish whether it needs to be filled. The following options might be available:

- reorganization of work and duties

- new patterns of overtime or shift working

- subcontracting

- using an agency.

If a vacancy exists consideration can then be given to whether it has to be filled internally or externally. Internal options include:

- promotion from within

- transferring current employees without promotion.

What is the job and who is the right type of person to fill it?

Defining the overall purpose or role of the job and the main tasks to be carried out is achieved through the written *job description*. The main issues to be covered in the job description are:

- the location of the job: for example, site, department, clinical directorate, locality resource group

- the title of the job

- the job title of the individual to whom the job holder is responsible

- the job grade

- the job title of any individuals responsible to the job holder
- brief description of overall job purpose
- the main tasks to be carried out by the job holder.

Distinguishing the right type of person is achieved through the formulation of a *personnel specification*. More specifically this sets out the qualifications, experience, and personal qualities required by the job holder. These requirements are intimately linked to the job description in that they should derive from an analysis of the knowledge and skills needed to carry out the job. Once the requirements have been identified, the person should be analysed under appropriate headings. This can be done in different ways. The two most common plans, those developed by Rodgers[5] and Munro Fraser[6], are set out below respectively.

The seven-point plan

1 Physical make-up
2 Attainments
3 General intelligence
4 Special aptitudes
5 Interests
6 Disposition
7 Circumstances.

The five-fold grading system

1 Impact on others
2 Acquired qualifications
3 Innate abilities
4 Motivation
5 Adjustment.

These or other plans are often refined to distinguish factors which are essential or desirable.

How do you attract the right people?

The most common means of attracting staff is through advertisements. According to Strike[3] advertisements might be placed in the following places:

- national and local newspapers
- recruitment agencies

- career services
- professional journals
- employment centres
- universities
- public notice boards
- internal vacancy bulletins.

The method of advertising used will depend on such factors as resources and costs, time to recruit, and the nature of the labour market (the type skills, professions, occupation groups sought).

How do you pick the right person?

Two principles should underpin the techniques used to select new employees; *reliability,* the extent to which a selection technique achieves consistency in what it is measuring; and *validity,* the extent to which the technique measures what it sets out to measure. Attempts have been made to achieve reliability and validity through the following selection techniques:

- application forms
- testing (trainability tests, attainment tests, personality tests)
- group selection and assessment centres
- references.

Interviewing remains the most common means of selection. It does have well established drawbacks related, for example, to the disproportionate influence impressions, potential subjectivity, and inconsistency in judgement. Steps can, however, be taken to minimize these drawbacks through:

- careful selection of the interview panel although in the case of medical appointments this is laid down by statute
- careful formulation of questions to avoid ambiguity and to ensure that the correct type of information is sought and elicited
- the standard application of questions
- the systematic recording of question answers.

These steps should aid recall, facilitate comparisons and help make more objective decisions, and help to subsequently justify choices.

Relevant employment law

Discrimination on grounds of sex

Care should be taken in recruiting and selecting not to discriminate on grounds of sex. Under the Sex Discrimination Act 1975 it is unlawful to discriminate against full time and part time workers on grounds of gender or marital status. The areas covered include discrimination in:

- advertising
- arrangement for determining who should be offered employment
- the terms on which employment is offered
- access to promotion, training, and career development (refer to the section on performance appraisal (p.28) which touches on the former two, and the section on labour utilization (p.37) which touches on the last).

Two types of unlawful discrimination are distinguished:

- direct discrimination – less favourable treatment on grounds of sex
- indirect discrimination – treatment which is discriminatory in practice, if not in a formal sense, in that a smaller proportion of a particular sex cannot comply or meet an employment condition in comparison with the other sex.

Sex discrimination is not unlawful where a person's sex is a 'genuine occupational qualification'. A specific set of circumstances is laid down where variable treatment is acceptable on grounds because of the nature of the post or work.

Discrimination on grounds of race

Care is also needed not to discriminate on grounds of race when recruiting and selecting. Under the Race Relations Act 1976 it is unlawful to discriminate against job applicants or existing employees on grounds of race. Those areas of employment where it is unlawful to discriminate are similar to those covered by the Sex Discrimination Act and include recruitment arrangements, job offers, promotion, and training opportunities. Discrimination on grounds of race is also defined in the same ways as for gender, i.e. direct and indirect.

Written particulars

When taking on new staff it should be noted that all employees employed for a month or more are entitled to a written statement covering a range of issues including:

- pay rate or scale
- holiday entitlement

- hours of work

- job title or brief job description.

Within a two month period further information must be provided including:

- sick pay terms and conditions

- pension details

- notice period

- rules on disciplinaries and grievances.

Performance management

Performance management can be defined as a set of integrated policies and practices which seek to enhance the pursuit of organizational objectives through a concentration on individual performance. More specifically Storey and Sisson identify three key elements to performance management:[7]

1 the setting of clear objectives for individual employees (these objectives are derived from the organization's strategy and a series of departmental purpose analyses)

2 formal monitoring of review and progress towards meeting objectives

3 utilization of the outcomes of the review process to reinforce desired behaviour through differential rewards and/or to identify training and development needs.

The elements of the performance management cycle are illustrated in Figure 2.3.[7]

Setting objectives

The objective setting process is problematic in a number of respects. Performance management is based on the assumption that corporate and departmental objectives should be translated into individual objectives. Yet these higher level objectives are sometimes unclear, contested, or in tension with one another. In addition, the need to invariably select a limited number of objectives ignores the complexity of peoples' working lives. Tasks are subtly linked and to pick out a few objectives may encourage the employees to focus on those to the neglect of others. There are also major difficulties setting measurable objectives for certain types of employees. As a means of addressing some of these difficulties, the distinction between objective measures of performance and subjective measures may be of use.

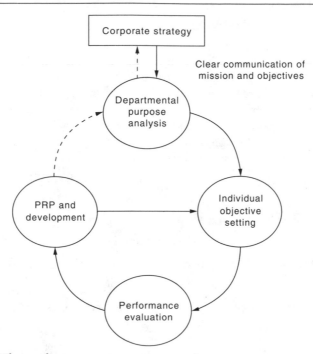

Figure 2.3: The performance management cycle.

Objective measures are reflected in relatively tangible and often numerical targets. Most organizations use at least some of these objectives. They are usually based upon quantitative data such as financial performance, productivity, output, or absenteeism. However, care has to be taken on the quality of these measures. They may appear robust but can often be more arbitrary than supposed. Mabey and Salaman note five conditions that might improve the quality of such measures:[8]

1 free from noise (influence by outside factors not relevant)

2 unable to be manipulated by insiders

3 straightforward to understand

4 inexpensive to collect

5 relevant, in the sense of reporting on the dimension of performance desired.

Subjective measures, although traditionally less popular because of difficulties in verification, nonetheless do greater justice to the complexities of performance. They are much more concerned with how and why tasks are performed. The challenge facing Trusts is to develop subjective measures which are consistently and systematically applied and which can also be audited.

Monitoring and reviewing performance

It is an essential characteristic of performance management that the evaluation of the employee's performance is not a once-a-year exercise. Regular meetings should take place throughout the year to modify individual objectives in the light of changed circumstances as well as to provide an opportunity for either the reporting manager or employee to provide positive or negative feedback on progress to date – in this way shocks may be avoided at the end of the year. However, the centrepiece of the evaluation process is the annual appraisal. Hiltrop and Sparrow[9] note that the appraisal interview should have the following broad aims:

- suggest ways in which the employee's good work can be continued and how he or she can achieve further improvement
- encourage the employee to discuss his or her strengths and weaknesses
- clarify how far agreed objectives have been met
- identify obstacles that are restricting performance
- produce an agreed plan of action that will lead to improved performance.

In deciding how to approach the appraisal a number of questions need to be addressed.

When will the appraisal be done?

Given that the appraisal has different purposes, consideration must be given to whether each will be pursued at the same time. It may well be that it is better to appraise for different reasons at different times. For example, employees may feel inhibited in discussing performance and potential if they know that they are being judged at the same time for reward.

Who will do the appraisal?

It is common for employees to be appraised by their line managers. However, not only may the employee's own assessment of him or herself also play an important part in the process (self assessment) but other interested parties may have much to contribute. For example, appraisal may involve peers – particularly important in relation to certain professional groups – and could involve not only peers but subordinates as well as superordinates (360 degree appraisal).

How should the appraisal be conducted?

Randall *et al.* have distinguished different appraisal interview styles:

- tell and sell: the manager spelling how and why the employee is performing in a given way

- tell and listen: the manager describing the employee's performance and then encouraging the employee to explain it and ways forward
- listen and support: the manager talking out the problem when the employee raises a number of complaints
- joint problem solving: a two way process of finding agreed ways forward in improving the employee's performance.

Utilizing the interview

The appraisal can have three main purposes each with a different outcome (Table 2.2).

Table 2.2: Purposes of an appraisal interview

Approach	Purpose	Outcome
Current performance	Reviewing performance in the current job	Finding ways to address agreed concerns or weaknesses in current performance; these might include training programmes, more managerial support, and additional resources
Career development	Reviewing potential, that is future career and promotion prospects	Finding ways to ensure that the potential is realized through, e.g., development programmes, exposure to a greater range of experiences or work
Reward	Reviewing reward	Findings can input into decisions on whether the individual should be promoted and are more likely to inform decisions on pay increases

Relevant employment law

As stressed above it should be noted that under the Sex and Race Discrimination Acts it is unlawful to discriminate on grounds of sex and race in determining promotion and training opportunities (see above). This should be borne in mind, for example, when dealing with the outcomes of the appraisal process and all stages of the performance management process.

Reward systems

Types of reward

Rewards can be distinguished according to whether they are intrinsic or extrinsic and whether they are individually based or system wide. Four types can therefore be noted (Table 2.3).

Table 2.3: Reward systems

	Extrinsic	Intrinsic
System-wide	Organization or sector based fringe benefits such as insurance or discount schemes, luncheon vouchers, loans, subsidized mortgages, general pay increase	Pride in the organization as reflected in the general quality of service provision
Individual	Merit based pay increases or bonuses	Feelings of self-fulfilment related to task undertaken or service provided

These types of reward are clearly not mutually exclusive. However, the attention of policy makers and managers has tended to focus upon extrinsic monetary rewards, in other words, pay.

The traditional approach to pay in the NHS

Pay in the NHS has traditionally been governed by a high degree of standardization through central Whitley and Pay Review Body machinery. Views on this traditional model vary. Strike[3] suggests it is perceived as:

- bureaucratic

- binding

- inflexible

- unresponsive

- over regulating.

Such a view is based upon the suggestion that the traditional system produced:

- uniform and rigid forms of work organization

- fixed occupations

- rigid job and grade categories

- set working hours

- dictated rates of pay

- detained terms and conditions of service.

On the other hand, given employee sensitivity to pay and other conditions, and the need to be publicly accountable for pay increases, the traditional system has been based upon a fair degree of consensus, has produced relative stability in industrial relations terms, and has been resource efficient in terms of the time and effort devoted to determining pay.

Within certain constraints, in particular the rights of staff transferred to the Trust to retain Whitley terms and conditions, Trusts as employers now have discretion to develop their own pay systems. In deciding on how to exercise this discretion, a number of questions need to be addressed.

What are the pay objectives?

Pay can be used to pursue a range of objectives. These have often been based on the need to:

- recruit

- retain

- motivate.

However, a much more extensive and refined list can be produced which includes:

- rewarding individual performance

- rewarding the group performance

- incentivizing the individual

- incentivizing the group

- establishing 'fair' differentials between occupations, i.e. rewarding job skills and responsibilities

- creating employee loyalty and commitment to the organization

- stimulating change in organizational values

- reinforcing change in organizational values

- ensuring stability and predictability in earnings

- ensuring simple and low cost pay administration.

Identifying pay goals clearly is crucial for they are not all compatible with one another. For example, the need to recruit and retain, in other words respond to labour market pressures, is in tension with a concern to reward the individual for his or her performance. Similarly simplicity, predictability, and low cost administration may not readily accord with the sophisticated schemes associated with incentivizing or rewarding the individual or group. Moreover, there is an implied tension between criteria for rewarding or incentivizing. Are these based upon the quantity or the quality of output?

What payment systems are available?

Once pay goals have been established, the next step is to consider which pay systems are best suited to pursue these goals. Mahoney's diagram in Figure 2.4 indicates the different contingencies upon which pay can be based. The three contingencies further pay goals in differing ways:[10]

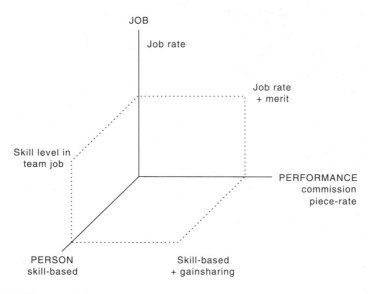

Figure 2.4: Pay contingencies.

Job: basing pay upon the job, usually through a job evaluation procedure, recognizes the bundle of skills and responsibilities that make up that job regardless of the individual who performs them. This provides clarity and predictability in reward and establishes fair differential between jobs.

Person: this approach to pay rewards the person for what they bring to the job in terms of their own qualifications, skills, and experience. Reflected in seniority based pay, or grades linked to professional qualifications, the pay objectives of predictability and clarity and encouraging perceptions of fairness are again to the fore.

Performance: this approach to pay is based upon how the individual or the team actually perform on the job. As a consequence it is concerned with reward and incentives. Pay may also be based on the performance of the organization and in this case there may an interest in encouraging a sense of 'corporate' loyalty and commitment.

It is clear from the diagram that different pay contingencies can be combined. Thus, an element of pay can be related to the job and supplemented by a person or performance related element. However, there is a danger that these uses of different contingencies may distort or obscure the underlying goals in the eyes of the recipient. Moreover, too much weight may be placed upon pay as a management tool to the neglect of personnel mechanisms.

Is the pay system right for us?

The final question which must be addressed is whether the pay system is appropriate given the characteristics of the Trust. In other words, while a pay system might be seen as the way to pursue selected goals, it is simply not 'right for us'. The characteristics that may be important in this respect include:

- the kinds of occupational groups found in Trusts; for example, in the case of some groups, say nurses, individual performance may be very difficult to measure, undermining the viability of individual performance related pay
- the prevailing attitudes and values within the NHS generally as well as within specific Trusts; in this respect the ingrained way of determining pay as reflected in employee expectations and assumptions cannot readily be ignored in seeking the 'right' pay system
- the nature of the work carried out; in the NHS work is perhaps based more upon the team than the individual.

Relevant employment law

Equal pay

In developing new pay structures and systems, it should be noted that under the Equal Pay Act 1970, men and women in full and part time employment are entitled to equal treatment in relation to terms and conditions of employment in the following circumstances:

- when they are employed in the same or broadly similar work
- when a job evaluation scheme has rated their work as equivalent
- if the work is of equal value (although in this case an employer can claim the difference in pay is linked to a 'material factor' unrelated to gender, e.g. age, experience).

Communication

What types of communication are available?

Communication within the Trust can take different forms. These differences are based upon the:

- direction of communication: whether it is upwards, downwards or two-way the channel of communication: e.g. whether it is written or verbal

- 'unit' of communication: i.e. whether communication is with the individual or the group
- substance of communication: i.e. whether it is the communication of factual information, ideas, views, problems, or solutions.

Table 2.4, (a modified version of a table produced by Hyman and Mason[11]) sets out the main forms of communication.

Table 2.4: Main forms of communication

Method	Flow	Goal
Group		
Briefing groups	Downward	Team communication
Chairman's forum	Downward	Information dissemination
Employee reports	Downward	Information dissemination
Newspapers and newsletter	Downward/two-way	Information dissemination Expression of views
Quality circles	Upward/two-way	Quality ethos Diagnostic improvements
Departmental meetings	Downward/two-way	Information dissemination Expression of views
Individual		
Counselling and mentoring	Two-way	Employee development Welfare
Attitude surveys	Upward	Temperature taking
Suggestion schemes	Upward	Diagnostic improvements

Most of the types of communication highlighted in this table are self explanatory. However a few require further elaboration.

Briefing group or team briefing – in its most popular form this comprises a process of cascading information down the organization. The standard information is provided at the top of the organization and is adapted by the departmental, sectional, or ward manager who ensures that it is relevant and accessible to his or her staff.

Employee Reports are usually prepared by the Board specifically for employees to inform them of ongoing strategy developments.

Quality circles are essentially work- or task-centred forms of communication whereby employees can provide ideas or suggestions for improvement related to the nature of service provision and its associated procedures and activities.

Attitude surveys are usually based upon the administration of a structured questionnaire sent to a sample of staff; these are conducted at one or two yearly intervals to monitor changes in employees' views on a range of selected subjects.

Why communicate?

As with pay, the goals of communication are varied and the choice of technique may well depend on purpose. This relationship is in part indicated in Table 2.4. More specifically, Torrington and Hall highlight the differing goals underpinning downward and upward communication.[12] They note that downward communication is important because:

- it enables decisions taken by managers to result in action by employees
- it ensures that this action is consistent and coordinated
- costs should be reduced because fewer mistakes are made
- it may stimulate greater employee commitment and as a result better customer service
- from all these should stem greater organizational effectiveness.

They note that upward communication is important because:

- it helps managers to understand employees' business and personal concerns
- it helps managers to keep more in touch with employees' attitudes and values
- it can alert managers to potential problems
- it can provide managers with workable solutions to problems
- it can provide managers with the information they need for decision making
- it helps employees to feel that they are participating and contributing and can encourage motivation and commitment
- it provides some feedback on the effectiveness of downward communication, and ideas on how it may be improved.

How do you communicate effectively?

The effectiveness of communication can be undermined by a number of factors. The use of jargon, for example, is likely to undermine effective communication. If the message being conveyed does not accord with the recipient's experiences, sometimes referred to as cognitive dissonance, its impact is similarly likely to be diluted. Problems will also arise if the person doing the communication lacks conviction or commitment. Platts and Southall provided a comprehensive list of the principles characterizing effective communication:[13]

- top management commitment
- sufficient time and money
- planned and deliberate

- understandable
- systematic
- regular and well timed
- relevant
- right amount
- supported by training
- support in preparation
- agreed objectives
- think message then medium
- open and honest
- within the recipients' horizons
- interesting, significant
- constantly reinforced content.

Relevant employment law

The law does not have much to say on communication. However, it is important in the following two areas.

Consultation on redundancies

Recognized trade unions or, in their absence, other employee representatives, have a right to be consulted about prospective redundancies. If 100 or more redundancies are involved consultation must take place at least 90 days before the first dismissal; if between 20 and 99 redundancies, 30 days. The employer must give information on the reasons for the redundancies and on the numbers and posts involved.

Health and safety

The Health and Safety at Work Act 1974 places a duty on employers to provide 'such information, instruction, training, and supervision as is necessary to ensure, so far as is reasonably practicable, the health and safety at work of employees'. This has been reinforced by the Health and Safety Information for Employees' Regulations 1989, which require employers to bring to the attention of their employees information relating to general requirements and duties under health and safety law.

It is of course important to note that legislative requirements related to health and safety at work are much broader than information giving. The 1974 Act gives employers a duty to ensure, so far as is reasonably practicable, the health and safety at work of their employees. This Act is essentially an enabling piece of legislation with substantive changes in the main being induced by regulation. While space does not permit full details of these regulations, a list of the main ones indicates the types of areas covered and, in so doing, where it might be necessary to seek expert advice. Key health and safety regulations include:

- reporting of injuries, diseases, and dangerous occurrences regulations

- health and safety (first aid) regulations

- chemicals (hazards information and packaging for supply) regulations

- control of substances hazardous to health

- notification of new substances regulations

- health and safety (display screen equipment) regulations

- workplace (health, safety, and welfare) regulations (covers heating, lighting, and general welfare facilities).

Labour utilization

Labour utilization involves the efficient and effective use of staff through careful structuring and design of jobs within the Trust and a careful balancing of skills and competencies within the Trust workforce as a whole. The following areas linked to labour utilization have emerged as significant within the health service:

- labour flexibility

- skill mix

- grade mix.

Labour flexibility

There are two main forms of labour flexibility: numerical and functional flexibility. Numerical flexibility is based upon the ability of the employing organization to vary the numbers of staff in response to shifting product market demand and fluctuating financial circumstances. Such flexibility is seen as being achieved through the use of:

- fixed term contracts

- casual or temporary workers

- part timers

- job sharers.

An example of such flexibility in the health service would be the employment of, say, nurses on fixed term contracts covering the period of funding for a waiting list initiative; in these circumstances renewal of staff contracts might depend on renewal of funding.

Functional flexibility relates to the adaptability of employees within or between jobs. Staff might be flexible in a 'horizontal' sense, that is, able to perform a broader range of different tasks at a similar skill level. They may also be flexible in 'vertical' terms, able to carry out work involving lesser or more likely slightly greater skills and responsibility than their current jobs require.

A further form of flexibility is 'distancing'. This involves the organization using an outside agent or contractor to provide certain services. While the host organization retains ultimate responsibility for these services, operational decisions, including those related to the employment and deployment of staff are the province of this outside body. The relationship between host organization and outside agent or contractor is usually regulated by a contract with clear service specifications. In the health service, the use of contractors to provide certain ancillary services would be an example of 'distancing'.

The flexible firm model (Figure 2.5) highlights the way in which these different forms of flexibility might be related.[14] As presented in this model, functional flexibility is associated with the organization's core employees, those you wish to nurture and retain while functional flexibility is equated with peripheral workers who are more expendable.

Presented in this way the terms 'core' and 'periphery' are somewhat problematic in that numerically flexible groups may well be involved in the organization's central or core activities. However, the distinction between core and periphery certainly forces the organization to consider how it will treat the respective groups:

- will different criteria be used to recruit core and peripheral groups or will the organization be looking for the same characteristics?

- do you communicate with these groups differently or in the same way?

- how do you ensure the loyalty, commitment, and motivation of peripheral employees to the organization?

- what mechanisms do you use to develop core staff?

Skill mix

Skill mix has been defined as: 'the balance between trained and untrained, qualified and unqualified, and supervisory and operative staff within a service area as well as different staff groups. The optimum skill mix is achieved when a

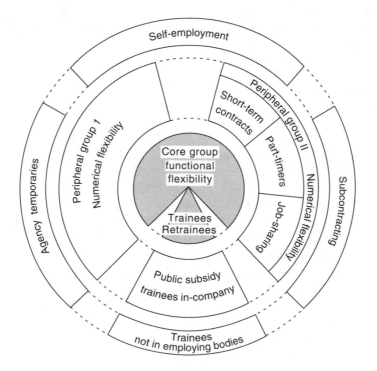

Figure 2.5: The flexible firm model.[14]

desired standard of service is provided at the minimum cost, which is consistent with the efficient deployment of trained, qualified, and supervisory personnel and the maximization of contribution of all staff' (North East Thames Regional Heath Authority, 1992). It has been noted[15] that a number of developments have stimulated skill mix reviews including:

- increased day surgery
- more rapid patient turnover in hospitals
- changing medical and clinical practice
- Project 2000
- The Patient's Charter
- The NHS and Community Act
- increasing emphasis on community care
- the declining number of NHS continuing care beds for elderly people.

There is no set formula for determining an ideal skill mix in any clinical setting although crude methodologies are sometimes used. Most skill mix methodologies attempt to:

- identify existing workload
- identify existing staffing levels and skills
- minimize staffing costs
- review work undertaken in the area
- adjust skill mix or staffing to reflect work actually undertaken.

Grade mix

Grade mix is a more narrowly focused activity than skill mix and focuses on the number of staff required within different grades. Grades are defined by a bundle of skills and responsibilities. In a grade mix review attention is given to whether the distribution of staff within grades matches the organizational, directorate, or ward needs in terms of required skills and responsibilities. As Strike notes, 'as with skill mix, cost should not be incurred for expertise that will not be utilized, so higher grades within services needs to be utilized to be justifiable'.[3] He goes on to note that grade issues can be progressed through:

- review of job descriptions against grade definitions
- workforce planning
- re-grading
- protection of pay (for those who may have to be downgraded)
- re-deployment (within the organization to ensure the expertise associated with particular grades is utilized where it is needed within the Trust).

Relevant employment law

Moves towards greater flexibility and a focus upon skill or grade mix may involve reducing workforce numbers and even moving groups of employees out of the organization. Given these possibilities the following areas of employment law become relevant.

Unfair dismissal

An employee who has been employed continuously for two years or more has a statutory right not be unfairly dismissed by his or her employer. (At the time of writing the two year time limit is being challenged under EC law so check it still pertains.) To establish whether the dismissal is unfair the following steps are followed (Table 2.5).

Table 2.5: Process for establishing unfair dismissal

1	Has there been a dismissal?	Termination of contract with *or* without notice Termination of a fixed term contract without renewal An employee terminates the contract because of the employer's conduct – sometimes called 'constructive dismissal'
2	What is the reason for the dismissal?	Capability or qualification of the employee Employee conduct Redundancy Legal restriction making continued employment impossible 'Some other substantial reason' justifying dismissal It is automatically unfair to dismiss an employee for membership or non-membership of a union and on the grounds of pregnancy
3	Was dismissal for this reason justifiable in the circumstances?	Clearly there are no hard and fast rules for circumstances which will vary according to each case. Nonetheless, decisions reached have established the importance of following procedures prior to dismissal. In other words, for a dismissal to be deemed fair it is important for organizations to have a 'fair' disciplinary procedure and to follow it

Redundancy pay

An employee who has been continuously employed for at least two years has a statutory entitlement to a redundancy payment. Dismissal is defined in the same way as for unfair dismissal. An employer can escape liability if 'suitable alternative employment is offered'. Statutory redundancy payments are calculated on the basis of length of service and there are upper limit payments.

Transfer of undertakings

The Transfer of Undertakings Regulations are particularly important in the context of competitive tendering which might result in outsourcing or externalization of services. The nature of the trade or undertaking transferred has been defined broadly and in all probability would cover tendered NHS services. Where there has been a transfer the new employer is required to observe all terms and conditions which applied to the employees in the transferred organization, other than terms related to the occupational pension schemes.

Conclusion

The management of staff is crucial to the efficiency and effectiveness of NHS Trusts. In recent years, Trusts have been given greater control of the levers and processes governing the management of staff. Moreover within Trusts, staff management has become an increasingly important part of the consultants' job as personnel responsibilities have been devolved to clinical directorates.

At the same time, staff management remains a complex and difficult area of activity. Trusts are still influenced and constrained in human resource management terms by a range of external forces including central government policies, NHS Executive initiatives, national union and professional association goals and campaigns, as well as by legal frameworks. Furthermore, the discrete human resource management policy areas require considerable knowledge on various techniques and procedures.

This chapter has been designed to help clinical directors and their colleagues steer a course through these complexities and difficulties. It has sought to:

- help identify the technical and procedural options available for each of the personnel policy areas

- provide some guidance on the criteria to be used in choosing between these options

- highlight some of the skills, knowledge, and attitudes needed to put the chosen option into practice

- distinguish some of the operational problems that might arise and how to deal with them.

It must be reiterated, however, that human resource management is a management activity which has many hidden traps. While the management of staff is sometimes seen as an every day activity, regulated by exercise of common sense and the application of general inter-personal skills, in practice it is a highly sophisticated world. The secret may lie as much in recognizing your limits as well as your abilities. This chapter has provided signposts to what is needed to manage staff; consultants should be prepared to seek further help and advice from within and beyond the Trust if difficulties arise in living up to these needs.

References

1 Audit Commission. (1994) *Trusting to the future*. Audit Commission.
2 Armstrong M. (1992) *Strategies for Human Resource Management*. Kogan Page.

3 Purcell J. (1991) *The impact of corporate strategy on MRM*. In: *New perspectives on MRM* (ed.) J Storey. Routledge.
4 Strike A. (1995) *Human resources in health care*. Blackwell Science.
5 Rodgers A. (1952) *The seven point plan*. NIIP.
6 Munro Fraser J. (1966) *Employment interviewing*. MacDonald and Evans.
7 Storey J and Sisson R. (1993) *Managing HR and IR*. Open University.
8 Mabey C and Salaman G. (1995) *Strategic HRM*. Blackwell.
9 Hiltrop J and Sparrow P. (1994) *European HRM in translation*. Prentice Hall.
10 Mahoney T. (1992) *Multiple pay contingencies*. In: *Human resource strategies* (ed.) G. Salamon. Sage.
11 Hyman J and Mason R. (1996) *Worker participation and involvement*. Sage.
12 Torrington D and Hall L. (1991) *Personnel management: a new approach*. Prentice Hall.
13 Platts M and Southall I. (1992) In: *Employee communication and effective involvement in strategies for HRM* (ed.) M Armstrong. Coopers and Lybrand.
14 Atkinson J and Meager N. (1986) *Changing patterns of work*. NEDO.
15 Royal College of Nursing. (1992) *Skill and grade mix*. RCN.

Further reading

Croner's Reference Book for Employers. Croner.
The Arbitration Conciliation Advisory Service (ACAS) publishes advisory booklets on most of the subjects covered in this chapter. It also has regional inquiry points which provide information to employment queries free of charge.

Negotiating: a five step approach to the negotiation of health care contracts

Sid Jennings

> We live in an age of negotiating. Almost all aspects of our lives are subject to some form of negotiation. Everybody negotiates, sometimes several times a day. We are so used to negotiating that we do not realize what we are doing
>
> Kennedy *et al.*[1]

The above quotation is relevant to all who work in the NHS; everyone from the most senior administrators to the most junior members of staff get involved in negotiations. Clinicians are no different to anyone else. They have always negotiated with each other and with other groups of staff but recent developments now require many of them to negotiate vitally important health care contracts with external customers. Yet very few of them have been provided with the necessary skills to carry out the role of negotiator effectively. The omission will be addressed in this chapter.

If negotiation is so commonplace, then what is it? A useful definition is provided by Fowler: 'Negotiation is a process of interaction, by which two or more parties who need to be jointly involved in an outcome but who initially have different objectives, seek by argument and persuasion, to resolve their differences in order to achieve a mutually acceptable solution'.[2] From this, it can be seen that negotiation is a method of resolving differences which is chosen by parties that are to some extent interdependent. Here we are going to focus upon the use of negotiation to resolve differences that exist between the providers and purchasers of health care facilities. Although both may share a commitment to high quality health care provisions being available to everyone through the NHS, when the providers and purchasers get together to determine the specific terms of a particular health care contract, clear differences can be expected to emerge as to the exact nature of the service to be provided and the actual cost attached to it.

Outlined below is a framework for negotiation which provides guidelines for hospital clinicians required to negotiate health care contracts. In the examples used to illustrate the various points made, it is assumed that the clinicians are negotiating with representatives of a large GP fundholder group. The framework provided is divided into a preparation stage (steps 1–3), and a negotiation stage (steps 4 and 5). Although it has been written for clinicians it is equally relevant for other groups, both inside and outside of the NHS, and can be applied to a wide range of commercial negotiations.

The preparation stage (steps 1–3)

What you do at this stage will determine the course and quite probably the outcome of the negotiation. Research shows that a key factor separating the skilled and the pedestrian negotiators is the way in which they prepare and plan their sessions.

Steele *et al.*[3]

Step 1: identify the issues, decide priorities, and determine bargaining opportunities

i *Identify the issues*

It is important to identify all of the issues that are likely to be raised during the negotiation. These include not only those issues which you intend to raise on behalf of the hospital but also additional issues which might be raised by the GP fundholders. This is important because if you arrive at the negotiating table with a brief prepared solely around your own concerns then you will be ill-prepared to respond to demands on unconsidered issues tabled by the other party. In this situation, you can either adjourn or postpone the negotiation in order to gain time to assess your position on these issues, or you can respond at the table and risk adopting an ill-thought out position which might later prove to have been counterproductive to your interests. Neither of these alternatives is ideal.

If you prepare thoroughly then you should be able to identify with a reasonable degree of confidence the key negotiating issues that will be raised. If you want to be certain that you have read the situation accurately, you could contact the other party and agree the issues for discussion prior to the negotiation meeting. Once you have identified the relevant issues you should begin to assemble appropriate information. To negotiate a health care contract firstly, you need to assemble general information on current conditions in the national and local health care markets. You need to know the supply and demand situation for the particular services to be negotiated, the strength of the competition that you are facing, and the terms and conditions relating to similar contracts agreed elsewhere. Secondly, you need to do your homework on the other party. You should seek answers to the following questions:

- what is the composition of the GP fundholder group?
- what is the extent of its resources?
- who are the most influential members?
- what are their most important concerns?
- how does the group take decisions?
- which other health care suppliers has it contracted with in the past?
- with whom does it have contracts at present?
- who are the negotiators and what is their status, authority, and experience?

ii *Decide priorities*

List all of the issues that are likely to be covered in the negotiation and decide whether they are of high, medium, or low priority to you. Now consider each of the issues from the perspective of the other party and assess the priority that the other party would allocate to the same issues (Box 3.1).

iii *Determine bargaining opportunities*

These arise when the parties accord different priorities to the issues to be negotiated. Each party will normally strive to achieve the best possible outcome on its high priority issues and to facilitate this, will be prepared to offer concessions on issues it perceives as less important. In an ideal situation, it may be possible for both parties to achieve near optimum settlements on each of their high priority issues. This can be illustrated by reference to the example in Box 3.1 where the respective priorities of the two parties were assessed as follows in Box 3.2. What the parties would be doing is trading concessions on issues of low priority to themselves (but of high priority to the other) for concessions on their high priority issues.

Step 2: determine your bargaining power and set your objectives

Here you need to determine whether you are in a strong or a weak position relative to the other party. Only after you have carried out this assessment will you be in a position to set achievable objectives.

i *Determining bargaining power*

Rojot says that the 'bargaining power of a party will rest in its capacity to influence the outcomes of the negotiation toward its own goals' and that 'it can

Box 3.1: Example: deciding priorities

You represent a hospital about to negotiate a health care contract with a group of GP fundholders. Your hospital has an ambitious five year development programme and it is important that it increases significantly the numbers of patients currently being treated. In order to justify planned investment in new equipment and staff the hospital needs a guaranteed income stream over the coming years. Consequently, in your negotiations with the GPs you have allocated a high priority to the achievement of the maximum number of patients being referred by them. You want the contract to cover as wide a range of treatment categories as possible and ideally, to be for a three year period. Your current facilities are first class and your waiting lists are below the national average. Although you intend to seek the highest price you can get, if you are offered the going rate within the NHS for similar health care contracts then this would be acceptable to you.

You have allocated the following priorities to the issues to be negotiated as follows:

Your priorities

Number of patients supplied	(High)
Duration of contract	(High)
Range of treatment	(Medium)
Price	(Medium)
Quality of patient care	(Low)
Patient waiting time	(Low)

From your initial discussions with representatives of the other party it is clear that the GPs are seeking a high quality service at a competitive price. They asked a lot of questions about the length of your current waiting lists for many categories of treatment and indicated that they were looking for a hospital which could provide a comprehensive health care service. You developed a clear impression that if you could meet their requirements in respect of these items then there would be every possibility of them signing a substantial contract with you.

Based on the information you have, your assessment of their priorities is as follows:

Their priorities

Price	(High)
Patient waiting time	(High)
Quality of patient care	(High)
Range of treatment	(Medium)
Duration of contract	(Low)
Number of patients supplied	(Low)

Box 3.2: Example: determining bargaining opportunities

Hospital priorities	**GP priorities**
No. of patients (H)	Price (H)
Duration of contract (H)	Patient waiting time (H)
Range of treatment (M)	Quality of patient care (H)
Price (M)	Range of treatment (M)
Quality of patient care (L)	Duration of contract (L)
Patient waiting time (L)	No. of patients (L)
H = high, M = medium, L = low	

In the above situation, the hospital negotiators could table an offer such as: 'If you were prepared to guarantee us a high volume of patient referrals over the next three years then we would undertake to provide a first class service and to minimize waiting time before patients receive treatment'. Alternatively, the GPs might say: 'If you agree to meet the price we are asking then we would consider an exclusive contract with your hospital'.

---

also be expressed as the capacity of A to obtain from B what B would not have given or done without A's pressure'.[4] Hence, the party with the greater bargaining power is in a position to exert more influence on the process and outcome of a negotiation. Is this important? Yes, because as Atkinson points out 'If there is a significant imbalance in power between the parties, it will tend to be exploited'.[5] Therefore it is important to determine the balance of power between the parties before entering into negotiation.

How can you calculate whether your position is strong or weak? Winkler provides guidance in this: 'Power is based upon the damage which results if the parties do not agree. If one party is likely to suffer no effective damage, while the other will lose out badly, the first party is strong and the second is weak . . . (this) has to do with the quality and range of options available to each party in the event of the deal breaking down'.[6]

This can be illustrated by reference to negotiations taking place between a hospital and GP fundholders. The hospital will be in a strong position if:

- it has very little spare capacity for additional patients and can afford to turn away business
- if it does not have to compete for the business because there is a lack of alternate health care providers locally
- its reputation is high and the GPs are keen that their patients receive treatment at that particular hospital
- the GP fundholders are under pressure to sign an agreement quickly.

Conversely, the GP fundholders will be in a strong position if:

- the hospital has a lot of under-utilized capacity and has to attract more patients
- there are several hospitals locally in competition for their patients
- the amount of business offered by the GPs is such that the hospital cannot afford to miss out on it
- they do not need to reach agreement quickly whereas the hospital is under pressure to do so.

When evaluating your (and their) bargaining power the key questions to ask are:

- if they fail to reach agreement with us, what alternative courses of action are open to them?
- if we fail to reach agreement with them, what alternative courses of action are open to us?

The relative attractiveness of the alternative courses of action available to the parties will greatly determine the balance of power between them.

ii *Setting objectives*

It is important to arrive at the negotiating table with clear objectives on the issues to be discussed. If you fail to think through beforehand what you need to achieve and what your bottom line is, it will be difficult to negotiate effectively. You will either have to adjourn to consider your position every time the other party tables a proposal, or resort to a 'seat of the pants' response there and then. Neither of these alternatives is satisfactory and both are likely to result in sub-optimal outcomes as far as your hospital's interests are concerned. You can greatly increase your chances of maximizing your benefits by setting targets at the preparation stage. This is done as follows.

For each of the issues to be discussed you should decide your optimum objective, realistic objective, and sticking point. The *optimum objective* is the most favourable agreement that you can hope to achieve. The *realistic objective* is not as good as the optimum but is the agreement realistically to be expected. The *sticking point* is the point at which you will make no further concessions and you will be prepared to break off the negotiation if agreement cannot be reached at this point. If a matter of principle is at stake and compromise is ruled out then the optimum, realistic, and sticking point may be identical.

The setting of objectives can be illustrated by again referring to negotiations that might take place between a hospital and a group of GP fundholders. The two parties are to meet to discuss a contract relating to a certain treatment involving relatively straightforward surgery. Both parties have done their homework and have determined that the price charged for this treatment in other hospitals ranges from

£570–£720. The GPs have indicated that they expect the treatment to be delivered promptly when the need for it arises. The negotiation will focus upon price and delivery and the objectives set by the two parties might be as shown in Table 3.1.

Table 3.1: Example: setting objectives

	GP fundholders		Hospital	
	Price	Delivery	Price	Delivery
Optimistic	£560	On demand	£700	At hospital's discretion
Realistic	£625	Within 2 weeks	£640	Within an agreed period
Sticking point	£680	Within 1 month	£595	Within 20 days

Clearly the parties should be able to agree a price and delivery period within the respective sticking points of the two parties. Thus a deal on price is possible within the range determined by the maximum the GPs will pay (£680) and the minimum the hospital will accept (£595). Similarly, a delivery period could be agreed somewhere from the maximum the GPs are prepared to wait (one month) and the minimum period the hospital is prepared to offer (20 days). Which party achieves the most favourable outcome will be dependent upon the expertise of the negotiators and the balance of bargaining power between them.

It is not unusual for the sticking points of the parties to be set at levels which exclude the possibility of agreement being reached. For example, if in the above situation the GP fundholders had decided that their maximum price was to be £585 and the hospital's minimum price remained at £595, then there would be no scope for a settlement. In these circumstances, unless one (or both) of the parties changes its sticking point an impasse will be reached and the negotiation will break down.

Once you have set your objectives you need to organize your team and develop a game plan.

Step 3: organize the team and decide the strategy

Although negotiations can be conducted on a one-to-one basis when important contracts are being discussed it is strongly recommended that a small team be set up to share the tasks involved. All members of the team should participate in the development of the strategy.

i *Organizing the team*

In a team there should be a minimum of three members to cover the key negotiating roles: the *leader*, *strategist*, and *recorder*.

The leader will normally be the person who has the authority to take decisions. The leader does most of the talking whilst following the agreed strategy in search of an agreement which meets the team's objectives.

The strategist monitors the progress of the negotiation and pays particular attention to the strategy and tactics of the other side. The strategist will normally only speak when invited to do so by the leader. However, if the leader gets into difficulty then the strategist may intervene to 'buy time' by summarizing the situation, by asking the other team to clarify its position, or by calling for an adjournment.

The recorder notes details of all proposals and any conditions which are tied to these. Apart from occasionally seeking confirmation that he/she has recorded correctly items tabled by the other party, the recorder should only speak if invited to do so by the leader.

Other persons in the team must have specific reasons for being there. For example you might choose to include additional clinicians or administrators to speak on certain of the issues to be discussed. If you decide to include specialists they must clearly understand the limits of their contribution and should only speak when invited to do so by the Leader. If someone cannot be trusted to stay within his/her allocated role then it is probably better to exclude them from the team. A 'loose cannon' can inflict a lot of damage to its own side!

Over-large teams should be avoided. The need to ensure effective team discipline suggests that ideally there should be no more than five or six members in the team.

During the negotiation it is important to ensure that each member of the team observes the following rules:

- do not interrupt the leader unless this is absolutely necessary

- do not break a silence if this is benefiting your side

- help out other members of your team if they are in difficulty

- do not show dissent with other members of your team

- keep to your agreed role, i.e. leader, strategist, recorder, specialist

- consistently follow the agreed strategy at all times.

Discipline is important for team cohesion and for it to be successful everyone's input during the negotiation should make a positive contribution to the achievement of objectives.

ii Deciding the strategy

You should decide whether you want to be in a win–win or win–lose situation. Differences in the characteristics of these two strategies are shown in Box 3.3.[7] If

---

Box 3.3: Negotiating strategy

WIN–WIN	WIN–LOSE
Pursue own goals at expense of other party	Pursue own goals in common with other party
Play cards close to the chest	Put all the cards on the table
Disguise or misrepresent own needs	Represent own needs accurately
Use threats and bluffs and try to keep the upper hand	Share information and treat the other side with mutual understanding
Attack other party's truthfulness and/or legitimacy	Accept the other party as telling the truth and representing a legitimate position
See negotiation as a battle that has to be won	See negotiation as a joint problem-solving exercise

---

you have judged that you are in a relatively weak position then there may be no alternative but to adopt the win–win approach because with win–lose you are almost certain to lose. However, if you are negotiating from a position of strength then you can adopt either approach and be confident of a satisfactory outcome. With win–lose you are almost certain to win and with win–win you should be in a position to ensure that you win significantly more than the other party if you choose to do so. When you are in a strong position your choice of strategy could be dependent upon whether you are seeking a longer-term relationship with the other party or whether you see the current negotiation as a one-off situation. If the latter applies, then you might choose to exploit your position of strength and force the other party into making every available concession. However, a word of warning:

> Only a dreamy idealist would argue that the party with a power advantage should not use it when they see the opportunity, but the short-term gain may become a long-term handicap; revenge is sweet.
>
> Torrington[8]

Hence, if you have occasion to negotiate with the other party again when the balance of power is against you, then you can expect no mercy. Also NHS networks are such that you could easily develop a reputation for ruthlessness which could result in purchasers of health care services boycotting your hospital and taking their business elsewhere.

Once you have decided your overall approach you must consider how the opening session of the negotiation is to be handled. In particular, you need to think about the agenda and the opening proposal.

The agenda

Control of the agenda can have an important impact upon the conduct and result of the negotiation. The party which controls the agenda is in a position to determine the issues which will be addressed (and those which will not!) as well as the order in which they will be dealt with. If you are allowed to set the agenda then you could choose to omit certain issues altogether and arrange discussion of the accepted issues in an order favourable to your own case. For example, you might choose to put your most important issues at the top of the agenda and theirs at the bottom. Alternatively, you might put one or two minor issues at the top of the agenda and make generous concessions on these in order to condition the other party into making reciprocal concessions on issues of greater concern to you.

Normally the organization hosting the meeting sets the agenda. If your team is not the host and no agenda has been set, then you should seize the initiative and propose your own agenda. If the other party has already set the agenda, then you should scrutinize this to ensure that it does not disadvantage your position. Negotiations over the agenda are an acceptable part of the bargaining process.

The opening proposal

This is important because it:

- determines one of the limits of the negotiation (when you table your optimum price for a health care contract this normally rules out the possibility of receiving a higher price)

- influences the bargaining range (i.e. the difference between the price you are offering and the price they are demanding)

- can lower the expectations of the other party and produce a more favourable settlement (negotiators who table high opening demands and defend their position vigorously, generally achieve better outcomes).

Is it better to get in first with your proposals or should you hold back? The answer is not straightforward as there are both advantages and disadvantages in getting in first. The main advantage in tabling the first demand/offer is that you can put forward your optimum position on each of the issues at stake and proceed to make it difficult for the other party to shift you from your stated position. Research indicates that the first demand/offer tabled during a negotiation tends to be more influential than the counter demand/offer. The disadvantage in getting in first is that in a situation of imperfect information you could easily pitch your demand too low or your offer too high. Also there is a danger that the other party might choose to play its cards close to the chest and reveal nothing about its own position whilst setting out to attack yours.

So how do you decide whether to open the bargaining or not? This will depend upon the degree of past experience the other party has in the negotiation of health care contracts. If he/she is relatively inexperienced in this activity then it is best to get in first and table an ambitious proposal. The other party will be uncertain as to whether you are being reasonable or not. However, if you are dealing with an experienced negotiator then it is probably better to encourage him/her to open the negotiation and to fully explore his/her position whilst revealing very little about your own.

You are now in a position to begin the negotiation proper.

The negotiation stage (steps 4 and 5)

> The successful negotiator is the individual who arrives at the negotiating table with sizeable demands, a sense of self-confidence, strongly committed to his opinions, willing to support those opinions with careful analysis, and prepared to grant relatively small concessions.
>
> Brandt[9]

Step 4: opening the negotiation

What happens in the opening session can have a major influence on the outcome of the negotiation. If this is handled successfully you can seize the initiative and put yourself in a very favourable position *vis-à-vis* the other party. To do this you must:

- create the climate which will be conducive to reaching agreement;
- establish your competitive advantage *vis-à-vis* other health care providers;
- lower the other party's expectations as to the likely terms of the agreement
- either table a proposal based on your optimum objectives on the issues at stake or invite the other party to table its own proposal.

Creating the climate

Lasting impressions are often formed within a few minutes of meeting someone for the first time. This must be borne in mind when negotiating with someone with whom you are not very well acquainted. Generally, negotiations are best conducted in a friendly, collaborative, and business-like manner and this requires an atmosphere of trust and respect between the negotiators. A couple of minutes of small talk on a current issue of joint concern within the NHS or even comments on the weather can be used to break the ice and to start the process of developing rapport.

Once greetings have been exchanged and the teams have been introduced, the business proper should begin. The starting point will normally be the agenda and the two parties will need to agree the objective of the meeting, identify the issues to be discussed, and decide the order in which they will be addressed. If differences emerge at this stage it is better to adopt a firm line but be prepared to show some flexibility if this is called for. Thus you should demonstrate that whilst you are willing to be reasonable you are not prepared to be a pushover. Minor skirmishes over the agenda can be quite useful in winning the respect of the other party. However, care must be taken to ensure that a tense or hostile climate does not develop. It is also good practice in your opening remarks to explain your concerns and acknowledge theirs whilst at the same time emphasizing the potential benefits for both parties which cooperation could bring. Words such as 'we', 'our', 'together', 'mutual', etc. should be used to identify joint interests and foster collaboration.

Establishing your competitive advantage

You need to convince the other party that there are very good reasons why it should come to an agreement with your hospital rather than take its business to one of your competitors. To do this you should emphasize your strengths *vis-à-vis* your immediate competitors and put forward selective comparisons to illustrate these. Examples of favourable comparisons might be the particular expertise of your clinicians, your investment in new buildings or equipment, the high quality of your patient care, your below average waiting lists, your competitive prices, or your geographic advantages. The more that you can convince the other party that it is in their interests to come to agreement with you, the better placed you will be to negotiate advantageous terms.

Lowering their expectations

Once you have created the right kind of climate and successfully sold the merits of your hospital, you must now set about structuring the expectations of the other party such that even before the hard negotiating starts the other party has begun to believe that its optimistic objectives on some of the issues are not going to be achievable. If you are successful in lowering the expectations of the other party you will simultaneously be improving your own chances of achieving an agreement close to your own optimistic settlement level.

If you are negotiating with the GP fundholder group you might set out to lower its expectations by making a number of assertions such as:

- the hospital has very little spare capacity and you are discussing what is available with several other potential customers

- top quality health care provisions are expensive but you refuse to lower your standards like some of your competitors have done

- the current prices charged for many categories of treatment are escalating faster than the rate of inflation and it is in their interest to reach agreement quickly to avoid price rises in the pipeline

- the NHS nationally is facing substantial rises in costs and all hospitals have no alternative but to pass these on to their customers.

Another ploy you might consider using is to mention in passing the terms and conditions of a recent contract (favourable to your hospital) which you negotiated with a different GP fundholder group. The intention being to implant in the minds of your opposing negotiators the parameters of the kind of agreement they might expect to achieve.

Structuring expectations is an integral part of the negotiation process and both parties can be expected to attempt it. If you are uneasy about the selective use of facts to present a biased view of reality in order to gain an advantage then you might bear in mind the following:

> Falsehood ceases to be a falsehood when it is understood on all sides that the truth is not expected to be spoken.
>
> Sir Henry Taylor (Statesman)

By now the preliminaries should be over and the scene set for the parties to state their positions.

Tabling a proposal

During your preparation you should have decided whether to open first or to invite the other party to do so. If you table your proposal first then you should speak with conviction and table your optimum position on each of the issues. You might emphasize the attractiveness of your proposal by using a selection of carefully chosen comparisons showing your offer in a favourable light in relation to the provisions of health care contracts negotiated elsewhere. You should beware of the other party attempting to undermine the credibility of your position without revealing its own. This can be done by refusing to revise any aspects of your proposal until the other party has tabled its own counter proposals. It is to be expected that the other party will declare your offer to be totally unacceptable and reject it unequivocally. This is part of the negotiation ritual and outright rejection should not be taken at its face value. If there are any important points of principle at stake relating to the issues being negotiated then you should state these when tabling your opening offer. For example: 'We are not prepared to differentiate between the service provided for your patients and those referred to us by other GPs' or 'If no bed is available the hospital must reserve the right to transfer a patient to another hospital at no additional cost to the fundholder'.

If they table their proposal first then you should assume that this is their optimum position on each of the issues and that they can be expected to make concessions as the negotiation progresses. Hence, you can anticipate that a proposal tabled by the other party will be ambitious. It should immediately be rejected in no uncertain terms. If you fail to be convincing in your rejection of their proposal then the other party will assume that it is perceived by you as reasonable and you will find it extremely difficult to shift the other party far from its initial position as the negotiation progresses.

How should you react if the initial proposal tabled by the other party is much more reasonable than you had anticipated beforehand? Even if the other party makes an offer which meets all of your optimum objectives it should be rejected as inadequate. Experience shows that if the parties in a negotiation settle too quickly both are likely to regret their actions later. On reflection, one party will feel that it demanded too little and the other will feel that it conceded too much. In these circumstances, both parties will be dissatisfied with the agreement reached. The need for both parties to participate in the ritual dance of negotiation in order to attain a satisfactory agreement is explained by Kniveton and Towers as follows:[10]

> The ritualistic steps of putting a case, considering it, arguing about it, pitching too high, all serve the function of ensuring that the negotiation is a lengthy procedure. There is ample opportunity for each side to pitch high and then feel their way slowly to an acceptable compromise without either side feeling that they have given too much. At the end both sides can legitimately appear exhausted and pleased that it has been a hard fight and that they both had to give some ground yet both have come out with an acceptable agreement.

It is quite normal for the process of tabling proposals to be accompanied by a subtle change in attitude between the parties. The friendly, cooperative mood which prevailed before the actual tabling, when the shared interests of the parties were very much to the fore, will now have been replaced by a much more formal, tense atmosphere with each party emphasizing its own interests and distancing itself from those of the other. Both parties will now be espousing strong commitment to their own proposals and demonstrating an unwillingness to compromise. Hence, the ritual of negotiation has brought about an apparent shift from a win–win to a win–lose situation.

When both parties have tabled their proposals then the parameters of the negotiation have been set. The range within which bargaining will take place has been determined and each party will now use its expertise to manoeuvre the other into making desirable concessions. Tactical ploys have a key role to play in the next step.

Step 5: manage the bargaining and finalize the agreement

This is the most crucial step of the negotiation. Even if your preparation was first class and you opened brilliantly, if you mismanage the hard bargaining that follows or fail to conclude the agreement satisfactorily, then all of your previous good work might count for nothing. The success or failure of the whole negotiation will be decided at this step.

i *Managing the bargaining*

This involves adopting appropriate behaviour and applying tactics to generate movement.

Appropriate behaviour

- Be business-like and keep in control.
- Adopt positive body language.
- Sit forward and maintain good eye contact with the other party.
- Be assertive but beware of being antagonistic.
- Follow your normal style of behaviour and do not attempt to be aggressive if you are not comfortable with this.
- Place due emphasis on the important points you wish to make.
- When you respond to points made by the other party, give yourself time to think and refuse to be hurried.
- Seek early acceptance of your key points.
- In the opening exchanges seek confirmation from the other party that it accepts any points of principle which you have tabled as well as key arguments around which you have built your proposal.

If you are successful in this then the negotiation should proceed on grounds favourable to yourself. If you cannot achieve acceptance of your points of principle/key arguments then be prepared to move the negotiation forward without abandoning them.

- Use probing questions.
- You need as much information as you can get from the other side concerning the issues at stake. Hence, you should seek:
  - general information on what their overall objectives are
  - specific information to clarify any proposals and arguments they put forward
  - feedback on their reaction to any proposals you have put forward.
- Always concentrate and listen to replies given to your questions in order to identify means of using their answers to your own advantage.
- Look to identify their key priorities and be alert for signals of possible movement from their stated position.

- Use silence to your advantage. If you ask a question or make a proposal which puts the other party on the spot and a silence ensues, do not break the silence, let it work to your advantage.

- Attack the issues not the people. Personal attacks on the credibility or integrity of members of the other team should be avoided because the most likely response will be retaliation. This can lead to a spiral of conflict and the negotiation will fall apart. So:

  NOT THIS 'You must be stupid if you think that we are prepared to be blackmailed by you!'

  BUT THIS 'We realize that the offer will be withdrawn if we do not meet the conditions attached to it. However, we cannot accept them in their present form.'

Tactics for movement

It is to be expected that both parties will initially seek to demonstrate a firm commitment to their opening positions and be reluctant to make major concessions early on in case this is interpreted as weakness. If this continues then the parties may find themselves in entrenched positions and the negotiation can drift into an impasse. To get out of this situation there are a number of negotiation tactics which can be applied. Rojot[4] describes a wide range of tactics and below are a selection of tried and tested ones which you might care to use. Some of the tactics listed are better suited to a win–win strategy and others fit better with win–lose.

- Call for an adjournment. Calling for an adjournment is a tactical ploy you might choose to use at several points during your negotiation with GP fundholders. In general, adjournments are useful when:
  - the GPs table a proposal which requires discussion by your team
  - new information becomes available which might justify a re-think of your objectives and strategy
  - the negotiation is stalled and both sides need time to take stock of the situation
  - discipline in your team breaks down and you need a break to restore order.
  During each adjournment your team should:
  - review progress against your initial objectives and revise them if necessary
  - review the effectiveness of your strategy to date
  - devise a game plan for the next bargaining session.

- Hold a corridor discussion. If the two parties have adopted entrenched positions and the negotiation appears deadlocked then one way forward might be to speak off the record, on a one-to-one basis, with the leader of the GP fundholders. Here you should try to determine the major impediments to progress and the minimum concession you could offer which could bring the negotiation back on track.

- Make a hypothetical offer. This is a conditional offer to test the water which can be withdrawn if you so desire. An example would be: 'If we were to agree to accept all of your NHS patients, would you be prepared to refer to us an agreed number of your private patients?' Link concessions by you on one issue to concessions by them on another issue: for example, 'We would be prepared to meet the price that you are asking if you were prepared to agree to our proposal for a three year contract'.

- Link together a number of issues in a package. Sometimes progress cannot be made by negotiating issues separately because the issues are related to each other. For example, you might not be prepared to agree a price until you know the number of patients involved and they won't specify the number of patients until they know what the guaranteed minimum waiting time will be. In instances of this kind, progress is often easier if several issues are grouped together and a package deal is negotiated.

- Negotiate issues separately. If you set out to negotiate a comprehensive contract covering a wide number of issues and fail then you could try negotiating an agreement on each issue separately. This way you might find that agreement on many of the issues is relatively straightforward and the outstanding difficult issues can be dealt with differently.

- Split the difference. If deadlock appears to be the situation even though the two parties are not too far apart then you might suggest splitting the difference between you. For example, 'You are demanding a maximum waiting time for treatment of two weeks and we have offered four weeks, so let us split the difference and agree to three weeks'.

- Offer a 'low cost' face saver. You could be in the position of having already won the argument but the other side being reluctant to signal agreement because it will come out of the negotiation having achieved very little. Here it can pay to be magnanimous and to offer a 'low cost' face saver to enable the other side to concede with dignity. For example, 'We are very pleased that you accept that we need to increase our charges and to show how much we value your business we will postpone the introduction of any price rises for thirty days'.

- Talk to the silent. If the leader of the other team is being particularly obstinate but from the body language of one (or more) of the side members it would appear that he/she is sympathetic to proposals which you have tabled, then you might choose to address this person directly. For example, 'Dr Johnson you know our hospital very well and I am sure that you agree with everything that I have said concerning the excellent quality of our health care facilities. You must see the merits in what I have proposed'. The tactic of addressing the silent is intended to break the unity of the other party and to undermine the stance adopted by its leader.

- Use a bluff or threat. This involves issuing a threat to impose some sort of sanction unless the other party makes a concession. For example, 'If you continue to insist that the outrageous price you have demanded is non-negotiable, we will call an end to our negotiation here now and now'. Only you will know for sure whether the threat is real or a bluff.

The tactics that you choose to adopt should pave the way for an agreement with the other party. If this is the case then it is important to address the detailed content of the agreement whilst it is fresh in the minds of both parties.

ii *Finalizing the agreement*

During the hard bargaining phase there will have been a tense atmosphere between the parties and at times the adrenaline would have been flowing freely. However, once provisional agreement is reached, the tension and stress tends to dissipate quickly and the parties become less guarded in their attitudes to each other. This situation can be exploited by an unprincipled negotiator attempting to unilaterally slip something additional into the agreement or by reinterpreting what had been agreed early in the negotiation. Hence, you should remain vigilant until the final wording of the contract has been completed.

The first step in this should take place immediately after the negotiation has ended. It is recommended that you follow Winkler's suggestion:[6] 'Summarize what has been agreed and get agreement that what has been summarized was agreed'. If the provisions of the agreement are in writing and both parties share a common understanding of what is written, then there should be no major problems later when the provisions of the contract are implemented.

References

1 Kennedy G, Benson J and McMillan J. (1980) *Managing negotiations*. Business Books Ltd.
2 Fowler A. (1986) *Effective negotiation*. Institute Of Personnel Management.
3 Steele P, Murphy J and Russill R. (1989) *It's a deal*. McGraw-Hill.
4 Rojot J. (1991) *Negotiation: from theory to practice*. MacMillan Press.
5 Atkinson G. (1990) *Negotiate the best deal*. Director Books.
6 Winkler J. (1985) *Bargaining for results*. Heinemann.
7 Johnston RW. (1985) In: Lewicki RJ and Litterer JA (eds). *Negotiations*. Irwin.
8 Torrington D. (1991) *Management face to face*. Prentice Hall.
9 Brandt FS. (1972) *The process of negotiation: strategies and tactics in industrial relations*. Industrial and Commercial Techniques Ltd.
10 Kniveton B and Towers B. (1978) *Training for negotiation*. Business Books.

Further reading

A very good book with a comprehensive coverage of the theory and practice of negotiation is Rojot J. (1991) *Negotiation: from theory to practice*. MacMillan Press Ltd.
A more basic guide to negotiation is Hiltrop JM and Udall S. (1995) *The essence of negotiation*. Prentice Hall.

Managing change

Sue Dopson

It is easy to think that the organization one works in and for, is unique in the changes it is experiencing. In fact, all organizations are affected by pressures for change to a greater or lesser extent. These include:

- increased competitive pressure

- more demanding customers

- political pressures

- demographic changes

- changing attitudes to authority

- changes in the labour market

- new information systems and, in the public sector

- changes in government financing.

Clearly these changes impact on organizations and individuals working within them, in very different ways. A simple and useful method for charting change was originally described by Kurt Lewin, a psychologist, who suggested that we could look at any organization, or any situation, as being held in balance or equilibrium between two sets of forces.[1] There are forces which are driving it, or seeking to change it, and forces that are restraining it. Figure 4.1 is what he calls a force-field analysis.

Lewin's model can be used to look at situations which are causing you problems; it might be a personal problem, or it might be a work-group problem, or an organizational problem. Lewin argues that if nothing is happening, it is because the restraining forces are equal to the driving forces. Examples of driving forces working on an organization can include: technological, economic, legal, social, political. The importance of such forces can be over-estimated. Change is not always desirable. However, listing the driving forces in a systematic way, that is, putting some kind of weight into them (longer and thicker lines) and

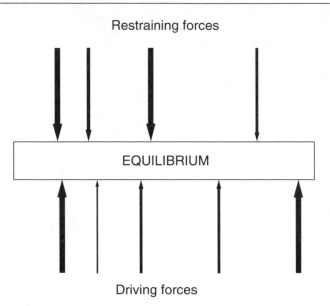

Figure 4.1: Force field analysis.

discussing your analysis with others, assists you and the people you work with to have a better overview of the situation you are facing. Too often organizations change regardless of any analysis. The force-field diagram reminds us that if we want to move the equilibrium forward, it is often easier to reduce the restraining forces than to add to the driving forces. It is therefore critical that people charged with management take a careful, considered look at the restraining forces to any change. If one does this, it might look like a daunting list of obstacles. Very often, the majority of restraining forces centre on the attitudes of the people involved. These attitudes clearly need to be understood and worked with if change is to be achieved.

A sensible first step when planning any change, is therefore, to list all the forces, both driving and restraining, actual and potential, and to use the people involved in the change to make up that list. Lewin also identified three crucial phases in the implementation of a change or innovation:

• unfreezing

• changing

• re-freezing.

Generally the unfreezing phase involves the softening of ideas and practices as part of getting people to be prepared to change. The changing period is really a period of persuasion to move from old ways of doing things to new ways. The re-freezing phase, according to Lewin, involves the new ways becoming accepted. Each of these phases clearly has its own particular set of problems. In the first phase, the issue is one of identifying and overcoming initial resistance. The second phase, the key issue is how to put the change into effect, which requires careful planning, and the third phase involves the institutionalization of change so that it is embraced by people and, in a sense, becomes part of the organization's culture. Before one attempts to introduce change, it is wise to think about the organizational culture the change is being introduced into. This begs the question, what is organizational culture?

Culture is a word often used in organizations to mean 'the way we do things around here'. Although this definition may feel intuitively correct, it underestimates the complexity of the concept. Figure 4.2 attempts to tease out this complexity.

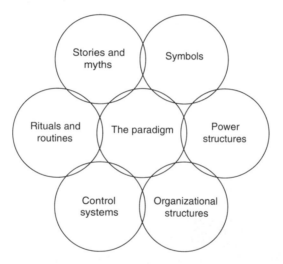

Figure 4.2: Organizational culture.

An organization's culture is made up of a combination of rituals, routine, stories, myths, and symbols that give very clear messages about what is seen as acceptable and unacceptable behaviour. However, an organization's culture is also influenced by the way in which power is distributed in the organization, and how work is structured and controlled. Culture is therefore a combination of values, structure, and power, that has implications for every aspect of an organization's operations and external relationships. We also know from research in this area that there are other important influences on cultures, including the history, traditions, and 'ownership' of the organization; its size, goals, and objectives; the technology it operates with, the nature of the workforce; and the environment in which it is situated.

anizational culture do you work in?

To help address this question we can usefully draw on a framework offered by Charles Handy,[2] represented in Figure 4.3, where organizational culture is discussed in terms of how formal it is and how centralized is its power.

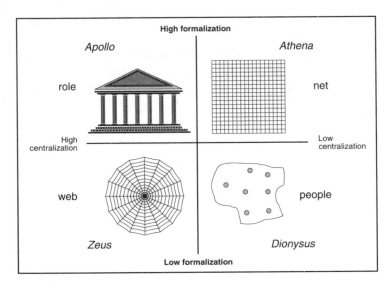

Figure 4.3: The culture quadrant.

The first of the cultures is the *power culture*, represented by Zeus, the god of power. Often found in small entrepreneurial organizations, it is pictured as a web because it depends on a central power source (a central figure or a coalition). It is a very political organization and decisions are taken largely on the outcome of a balance of influence rather than on procedural grounds. A lot of deal-making goes on. Decisions are usually made which will satisfy the central power source.

A power culture operates largely on the basis of anticipating the wishes of those seen to hold power. Control is often exercised by the centre through the selection of individuals and close control over resources. Individuals operating in a power culture will prosper if they are power oriented, politically minded, enjoy risk-taking, and can live with low security. People higher up the organization are often motivated by the drive for personal power and endeavour to build up close relationships with key figures. The lower ranks of the organization are often motivated by fear and dependency, although such fear can be mitigated by the benevolent paternalism of the 'boss'. Individuals working in this type of organization will be judged by results rather than by the way in which they achieve their goals. Often these cultures are tough and abrasive; they lead to high turnover, particularly amongst middle managers as they either fail or leave the hyper-competitive atmosphere. The claimed strength of this culture is that it can move very quickly if threatened, although this is clearly dependent on the individual/coalition at the centre. A major problem for this culture is growth. The web can break if it seeks to link too many activities, and struggles for dominance may result. The quality of the individual in the centre is crucial and this raises the question of succession. The sudden loss of the central power source can be a disaster. Generally, in this culture the employee resource is under-used and the boss resource over-used.

The second of Handy's cultural types is the *'role' culture*. This culture is often stereotyped as a bureaucracy. Its logo is a temple signifying its reliance on its pillars – the functions of the organization. Its patron god is Apollo, the god of reason. Where decisions are made depends on the amount of money involved and the extent to which the decision is not clear from the existing policies or procedures, usually defined or approved by committees. The work that goes on in the organization is controlled by procedures or rules, so this culture relies on job descriptions, procedures for communications, or rules for the settlement of disputes. The functions (pillars) are coordinated by a narrow band of senior management who represent the only personal coordination needed, since rules and guidelines guide the functions. Hierarchy is important, and people know their place. Position power is the major source of power, and personal power is frowned upon. In this culture the role or the job description is often more important than the individual who fills it. Performance over and above the role is not usually required and, indeed, can be disruptive. A well managed role culture offers security and predictability to the individual. The organization values and rewards consistency, order, and predictability. Those who stay within the rules feel safe from the exercise of arbitrary power. This may even give a certain freedom of action which would be constrained by uncertainty – the individual fear of capriciousness in the power culture.

The strength of this culture, argues Handy, lies where economy of scale is more important than flexibility. Role cultures are, however, slow to perceive the need to change, and slow to change when they do see the need, because very often they have relied on building up procedures and not people. This culture can be very frustrating for individuals who want to control their own work or who are power oriented. This type of organization is likely to succeed as long as it can operate in a stable environment; if it can control its environment by monopoly or the market is stable or its product life is a long one. Generally the role culture over-uses the talents and energies of the designers of systems and under-uses those of the 'doers'. A great deal of management ingenuity goes into the design and development of structures and systems which then limit and frustrate the ingenuity and initiative of the people who are charged with performing the work.

The third of Handy's cultural types is the *task culture*; represented by a net, this culture is linked to task force and project team environments. Athena, goddess of war and patron of the commando leader Odysseus, is its deity, standing as she does for the task force and the problem solver. A key characteristic is that it has some clearly articulated mission statement that is oriented to making a difference. Decisions are often made on the basis of expert knowledge and are geared towards advancing the mission. It is the mission statement that acts as the control and coordination mechanism.

Individuals know that they are unlikely to 'go wrong' if they pursue tasks associated with the mission. Influence and power are more widely dispersed. It is a team culture where outcomes should obliterate individual differences or status or style differences. The task culture assumes that people enjoy working at tasks that are rewarding and advance the shared purpose. The emphasis is on people being internally motivated; that is, the organization should provide opportunities for its members to use their talents and abilities in ways that are intrinsically satisfying and advance a purpose to which the individual is personally committed. There may be some room for individual professional interpretation of mission at a devolved level. A strength of the task culture is that it can evoke a sense of passion and commitment to work. The organization can empower people to learn and create new ways to achieve the mission ideals by making the appropriate resources available. However, a weakness of this culture is that in one's pursuit of the noble goals of the mission one can lose one's sense of balance, such that people exploit themselves in the service of the organization's purpose. Furthermore, this culture can be under-organized, relying on high motivation to overcome its deficiencies in structure, systems, and managing change. There may also be 'mission drift' if there is loose control of activity, or individuals' commitment is not congruent with the institution's.

The last of Handy's cultures is that of the *people culture*. It is unusual in that the individual is the starting point. If there is a structure or an organization, it is there to serve and assist the individuals within it. Dionysus is the patron god, the god of the self-oriented individual. Not many organizations can exist in this kind of culture since most have objectives over and above the collective objectives of those who comprise them. Furthermore, mechanisms are impossible in these cultures except by mutual consent.

Decisions are made on the basis of consensus. Coordination and control is achieved mainly through the selection of people who fit in with the existing individualistic culture. Influence is dispersed in this culture but power often lies with those who have relevant expertise. The ability to control one's work is the major source of motivation. At its best the people culture can evoke high commitment and can be supportive. However, its strength can be a major weakness in that people tend to avoid useful conflict in order to practise harmony and decisions can be taken covertly.

Organizations are rarely pure examples of these cultures. Rather a mixture exists, although Handy claims that there is usually a dominant cultural orientation. Considering the culture of your directorate is an important step before making change.

Why do people find change uncomfortable and resist it?

The most common reasons people resist change include a desire not to lose something of value, a misunderstanding of the change and its implications, a belief that the change does not make sense of the organization, a low tolerance for change, and a threat to our role in the organization. There are no magical ways of overcoming this kind of resistance; clearly it needs a lot of thought, a lot of care, a lot of sensitivity. Table 4.1 outlines some of the methods for dealing with resistance to change and their advantages and drawbacks.

We can improve our chance of successfully managing change if:

- we conduct some kind of organizational analysis that identifies the current situation problems and forces that are possible causes of those problems

- we analyse the factors relevant to producing the needed changes. Questions should include: who might resist the change, why, and how much; who has information that is needed to design the change; and whose cooperation is essential in implementing it?

- a change strategy is selected based on the previous analysis that considers issues of the organizational culture, the speed of change, amount of pre-planning, and degree of involvement of others needed

- we monitor the implementation process. No matter how good the change strategy and tactics inevitably something unexpected will eventually occur during implementation because of the complexity of changes that are being dealt with. Only by carefully monitoring the process, can the unexpected be identified in a timely fashion.

The checklist in Appendix 1 at the end of this chapter provides useful guidance in preparing for and implementing change.

Implications of change for managing the job

We discussed earlier the complexity of the health services and the rapid pace at which health services are changing. Clearly one consequence of this is that people working in the health service will be affected by these changes in terms

Table 4.1: Methods for dealing with resistance to change

Approach	Commonly used in situations	Advantages	Drawbacks
Education + communication	Where there is a lack of information or inaccurate information and analysis	Once persuaded, people will often help with the implementation of the change	Can be very time-consuming if lots of people are involved
Participation + involvement	Where the initiators do not have all the information they need to design the change, and where others have considerable power to resist	People who participate will be committed to implementing change, and any relevant information they have will be integrated into the change plan	Can be very time-consuming if participators design an inappropriate change
Facilitation + support	Where people are resisting because of adjustment problems	No other approach works as well with adjustment problems	Can be time-consuming, expensive, and still fail
Negotiation + agreement	Where someone or some group will clearly lose out in a change, and where that group has considerable power to resist	Sometimes it is a relatively easy way to avoid major resistance	Can be too expensive in many cases if it alerts others to negotiate for compliance
Manipulation + cooptation	Where other tactics will not work, or are too expensive	It can be a relatively quick and inexpensive solution to resistance problems	Can lead to future problems if people feel manipulated
Explicit + implicit coercion	Where speed is essential, and the change initiators possess considerable power	It is speedy, and can overcome any kind of resistance	Can be risky if it leaves people mad at the initiators

of what they do. It is, therefore, increasingly important for managers and professionals alike, to think very carefully about their jobs and how the job is changing or needs to change to cope with the new challenges change brings. One model that you might find helpful when considering what you do and how what you do is changing, is that proposed by Rosemary Stewart.[3] Stewart argues that job descriptions can, at best, only give a very limited picture of the job. They do not capture the reality of the changing situation, the complexity of relations with individuals and groups, nor the scope that exists for job holders to concentrate on particular aspects of the job. So each job holder has to discover what the job is like. This is a very personal discovery, as shown by the great variations in the kind of work that is done by people in similar jobs. People do jobs differently because their abilities vary, but also because they see different things as being important, interesting, or enjoyable. These variations in what people in a similar job can do, mean that there is considerable scope for individuals to choose what they do. The model of demands, constraints, and choices, developed by Stewart, based on her work observing and understanding what managers do, can be of use to the job holder more generally because it enables us to think about how best to use the opportunities that exist in a job, to decide what work you think is most important. The model is illustrated in Figure 4.4.

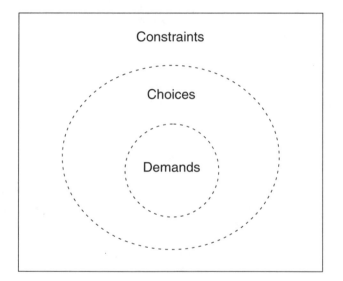

Figure 4.4: Demands, constraints and choices.

This figure shows the core of the job, labelled 'demands', that is, the work that anyone in the job would have to do, because they could not survive in the job unless it was done. These are the tasks that you cannot neglect or delegate. The figure also shows an outer boundary of constraints that limits what the job holder can do, and an area of choices that are the work that one person in the job may do and another may not. Use the simple task sheet in Appendix 2 (p. 74) to:

- consider the demands, constraints, and choices of your job

- of those that you have listed, decide what you would like to change

- list your ideas about how to change them.

Conclusion

This chapter has stressed the fact that change is a feature of your job. Managing change is difficult and there will often be unanticipated outcomes due to the complexity of your work. However, it will be much easier to handle if you plan for change and consider the possible implications.

References

1 Lewin K. (1958) Group decision and social change. In: *Readings in social psychology* (eds) E. Maccoby, T. Newcomb and E. Hartley. Methuen.
2 Handy C. (1985) *Understanding organisations*. Penguin.
3 Stewart R. (1992) *Managing today and tomorrow*. MacMillan.
4 (adapted from) Open University. (1994) *The effective manager: managing change*. Open University.

Appendix 1: Checklist for change[4]

Preparing for change

- seek to maintain an innovatory climate even when no specific changes are imminent
- be constantly alert to the possible need for change in the organization
- plan changes only to achieve some specific improvement in productivity and/or quality of working life – not on basis of whim, fashion, or resistable pressures from elsewhere
- identify the basic problem or opportunity
- change as little as is necessary to accomplish the desired improvement
- evaluate the driving and restraining forces before planning the change
- decide who else needs to be involved closely in planning the change
- invite their participation in planning the change
- anticipate the problems likely to be generated by the change.

Planning the change

- consider whether the benefits of the change are likely to outweigh the costs – in time, effort, resources, disruption, etc.
- plan the change in terms of what needs to be done, and in what order, and by whom

- cost the change in terms of time and resources needed (accounting if necessary for reduced productivity during the implementation phase) both to introduce the change and to maintain it

- draw up a realistic timetable for the change; from planning to 'institutionalization'

- ascertain the degree of support the change will have from your boss and from top management generally

- decide how the change will be monitored during the changing and re-freezing period

- work out criteria for judging whether people affected by the change are behaving appropriately and achieving the desired improvements

- devise early warning systems to detect difficulties, discontent, shortages, interferences, and unexpected snags

- keep a 'fire-fighting' reserve of time and resources to deal with problems whose precise timing and nature cannot be anticipated

- be prepared to modify the change where experience indicates improvements are possible.

Overcoming resistance

- consider how the change may interfere with or have repercussions for the work of other departments

- get the support of key opinion leaders whose attitudes could make or break the project

- identify people likely to be resistant to the change and the reasons for their resistance

- make sure potential resistors understand the potential benefits of the change

- be honest about any particular benefits that you personally will get from the change

- let potential resistors know how their opposition would affect the people expected to benefit from the change

- don't disguise your personal disappointment – let the resistors feel uncomfortable about it

- seek areas of agreement with resistors

- remain open to the possibility that your change may have drawbacks you have not yet recognized

- invite resistors to contribute to the change by suggesting modifications

- show genuine willingness to make justifiable modifications in line with their suggestions

- insist that emotional opposition be converted into constructive suggestions
- arrange for supporters of the change to be present in any important discussion where resistors are likely to be expressing dissent
- be reasonable at all times, and avoid getting into slanging matches with resistors
- if necessary, consider how resistors might be bought off
- consider whether resistors need to be manipulated or co-opted.

Appendix 2: Demands, constraints, and choices questionnaire

Figure 4.5: What kind of job do you have?

Write down for your job

1 Summary of the main purpose

2 Decide which of the five pictures in Figure 4.5 best describes your job

3 Write down the demands of your job: e.g. performance demands, behavioural demands

Which of these demands do you wish to change?

How might you go about achieving this change?

4 Write down the constraints of your job

Which of these constraints do you wish to change?

How might you go about achieving this change?

5 Identify the main choices you make in your job: e.g. what, how, when, who

Are there any other choices you feel you should take?

If your job has changed recently or is likely to change in the near future, tackle the following questions

6 How will the demands, constraints, and choices of your job change?

What actions must you take to manage these changes in your job?

Strategic planning

Noel Austin

If you can't plan it, you can't manage it

anon.

The preparation of business plans has taken its place as one of the annual rituals carried out by directorates and departments in Trusts; it is sometimes seen by those who have to do it as a disruptive and unnecessary process, imposed by senior managers, which obtrudes into the primary task of looking after patients. For that reason, it receives the minimum possible allocation of clinical time, is often carried out by business managers or by junior staff whose absence from the ward or the theatre is seen as having little impact, and is almost always done at the last moment. Occasionally it isn't done at all, since business planning is seen as the work of general managers and as having nothing to do with the delivery of care. In such circumstances it is done, under conditions of considerable stress, by hospital managers who have to fill the vacuum left by directorate inaction. Not surprisingly, their plans do not reflect a detailed understanding of directorate priorities and issues.

But what is the real justification for business planning? One of the consequences of the adoption of Trust status is that units which, until then, had had little opportunity to contribute to the development of district strategy, now find themselves with the responsibility for planning their own long-term development. The intention of the Resource Management Initiative, meanwhile, had been to bring about an improvement in management decision making by involving clinicians in decisions about the allocation of key resources. Taken together, these factors imply that not only is there a need for a substantial improvement in the quality of the long-term and short-term plans prepared by Trust management teams but also that these plans should take account of clinical priorities. Only in this way will it be possible to ensure that available resources are dedicated to getting the most effective and efficient patient care out of the resources available in the short and long term.

What is a business plan?

The very term 'business plan' is, in part, responsible for the reluctance of many clinicians to get involved in its development. In fact, a business plan is a document which sets out an organization's short and long-term plans, in terms of:

- what the organization intends to achieve, including the changes it intends to make
- how the organization intends to achieve it
- the starting point
- what resources it will need
- how it will satisfy its customers' needs
- what things can happen to interfere with the success of the plan
- what plans have been put into place to cope with unexpected and unwelcome developments.

This information is as valid for a directorate as it is for a Trust, a major industrial organization, or a corner shop. What is more, a real directorate business plan is not produced to satisfy 'the system'; it is an essential working document which every manager in the directorate uses to develop his own action plan and set priorities. However, a directorate business plan has other important functions:

- it sets out a statement of the financial and other resources which the directorate needs to deliver and what is expected of it by Trusts and commissioners
- it may be a promotional document used to inform and educate customers and potential customers about the services provided by the directorate
- it is a demonstration of the fact that the directorate recognizes that it consumes public money and is accountable to others for its short and long-term performance
- it shows junior staff that the directorate's management team has a clear understanding of where it is going and what the impact will be on its workforce.

Why have a business plan?

Professor Bernard Taylor of Henley Management College[1] carried out research into the reasons why major corporations prepared business plans; the key reasons quoted were:

- to provide a basis for the rational allocation of resources between and within operational units

- to provide a basis for diversification or repositioning the organization
- to make explicit expected changes in the external environment and the organization's responses to these changes
- to recognize and exploit changes in relevant technologies
- to provide a basis for coordination with other parts of the organization
- to provide a basis for contractual negotiations with major customers and suppliers, and with other parts of the organization

to which you may add, because you are spending public money:

- to provide evidence of your stewardship of the monies entrusted to you.

For whom is a business plan designed?

You will have recognized from the earlier discussion of the reasons for having a business plan that there are several groups of people who will take an interest in it. These include:

- yourselves (managers and staff)
- your colleagues in the Trust, directorate or department
- your clients and customers
- interest groups such as Community Health Councils (CHCs).

It will be clear from this short list that there will be different versions of the business plan for different readers. The starting point must always be that you are planning for your own benefit; it is only in this way that you will produce a living and useful business plan and such a plan is much more likely to provide the Trust's managers with an understanding of what you intend to do.

Who should produce a business plan?

The production of a useful and realistic business plan requires a great deal of hard work and the insights of many people. The team will include all the members of your directorate management team; however because so many people are involved in the provision of care to the patients of even a single specialty, the business plan needs the knowledge and insights of a range of other people, such as:

- clinical director
- business manager

- nurse manager (or other professional manager)
- general manager
- management accountant
- estates manager
- pharmacist
- therapist(s)
- radiologist
- pathologist(s)
- outpatients manager.

The work of this wide and disparate group of people must be orchestrated, and you should seek the support of the directorate business manager, or another manager to whom business planning is a familiar discipline, to undertake this task and pull together the final document.

Business plan components

Earlier in this chapter we referred to a business plan as including both long and short-term plans; we might more properly have referred to these as strategic and service plans. It is not uncommon for strategic and service plans to appear in separate documents, since there is no reason why they should be published at the same time. By and large, strategies change more slowly than service plans unless there have been some drastic changes in factors outside your control.

Time horizons

Strategic plans are not always long term (e.g. if a company is close to insolvency the only relevant strategy is to gain control of cash flow as soon as possible) but in the NHS it is conventional to think in terms of service plans as covering the next financial year and the strategy as covering the following four years, as required by the NHS Executive. However, if you are in a discipline, such as radiology or radiotherapy, where equipment has a life of ten or more years, you must think more than five years ahead.

Materiality

Materiality is a term borrowed from accounting but it is relevant to almost every aspect of a manager's job; it indicates that you should concentrate your management attention on those matters which are 'important, essential, relevant' (Concise Oxford Dictionary). With PCs and support from financial and management accountants it is possible to plan in a great deal of detail, creating a lot of work, and a spurious impression of accuracy. The point of planning is to help you manage, so plan in detail those things which:

- serve major markets

- consume significant resources

- incur significant costs

- include a significant risk.

In other words plan the important things in detail; an approximation will do for those things which aren't important.

Starting point

In the NHS, as in most branches of industry, commerce, and public service, it is now accepted that you must be guided, if not driven, by the needs and expectations of your customers. If this is so, then you cannot sensibly plan for the future without first finding out who those customers are, and what they need or expect. This is one of the tasks of marketing, and in an ideal world you would do some marketing before you started to prepare strategic and service plans. However, you do not live in an ideal world, and you may therefore find yourself in a position where you have to prepare your plans on the basis of available knowledge.

However, the rest of this chapter deals with marketing and strategic planning and Chapter 6 with service delivery planning in the expectation that you will, next year if not this, have the time to do things in the preferred order.

Marketing

> Marketing is so basic that it cannot be considered a separate function . . . It is the whole business seen from the point of view of its final result, that is, from the customer's point of view.
>
> Philip Kotler

> Marketing is human activity directed at satisfying needs and wants through exchange processes.
>
> Peter Drucker

These two definitions of marketing, by a marketing guru and a management guru respectively, are in wide circulation in industry and commerce but are not easy to relate to the NHS. We prefer to describe marketing as a discipline which helps you use your resources and the resources of others to create the greatest possible benefit for your customers, hence ensuring that they and you prosper. In order to do that, you have to find out who your customers are, or might be, and what they want or need, and then make the most effective use of your resources to satisfy those wants and needs.

> Satisfying the customer is a race without finish.
>
> Sony Corporation

You may conveniently think of marketing as being divided into two parts: strategic marketing, which is about finding out who your customers are and what they need or want, and then organizing yourselves to deliver it, and tactical marketing, which is about delivering what they need or want to your customers and seeking their views about what you have delivered. It will be apparent that since customers' needs and wants, competitive offerings, the environment, and customer perceptions are all subject to constant change, both strategic and tactical marketing are continuous processes; you must continually update yourselves on your customers and their views and change the way you do things in order to respond to them.

Those readers who have already been involved with quality initiatives will recognize similarities between marketing and quality, since both are about satisfying the needs of your customers. We shall develop this theme in chapter 9.

Customers and stakeholders

Before you apply marketing techniques to the management of your directorate, you must decide what you mean by a customer. The quality movement has a lot to teach you here, because it takes the view that everyone to whom you provide any kind of product or service is a customer. Most people would accept that, in the current NHS environment, this includes patients, GPs, both fundholding and non-fundholding, and other types of purchasers and commissioners, all referred to in the current marketing jargon as 'external customers' (Box 5.1).

Box 5.1: Some external customers

NHS patients
Private patients
Fundholding GPs
Non-fundholding GPs
Purchasers and commissioners
Social workers
Insurance companies
Other hospitals

However, if you focus your attention on the people and organizations with whom your directorate deal on a day-to-day basis, inside your Trust, you can add to this list other directorates, diagnostic departments, therapists, and estates departments, and many more; these are often referred to as 'internal customers' (Box 5.2).

Box 5.2: Some internal customers

Other directorates
Radiology
Pathology (or individual disciplines)
Physiotherapy
Occupational therapy
Speech therapy
Portering
Catering
Estates

Finally, there are people and organizations such as charities, pressure groups, patients' friends and relations, and the community at large, all of whom take a detailed interest in what you do and can bring pressure to bear on you to change what you deliver and how; these are commonly referred to as 'stakeholders' (Box 5.3).

How can you describe all these people as customers? Surely some of them are suppliers. This is true, of course, but in order for them to provide the products and services you need, they need things from you, whether they are request forms, or demand forecasts, or an effective means of *ad hoc* communication.

Box 5.3: Some stakeholders

CHCs
Mind
Macmillan Foundation
Hospital friends
Local authorities
The community

Market segmentation

It will by now be apparent that a complete list of all your customers would be very long; how can you cope with such a large number of customers without becoming submerged in a welter of complexity? Fortunately marketing has an answer to this conundrum, which is to:

- divide your customers into groups or 'market segments' with common needs and wants
- decide on which of these groups have the highest priority
- allocate your resources in proportion to the priority you give each group.

So how do you identify and describe the various market segments that you might wish to address? You will be familiar with some of the market segmentation criteria used in the fast moving consumer goods industry: socio-economic groups, which are primarily a measure of educational status and spending power, and family groups, such as single parent family, retired person, or retired couple, which provide more information about the preferences likely to be displayed by potential customers. There are many different ways of segmenting markets, and each organization tends to develop its own approach. However, these are all based on three key sets of variables, which are geography (where is the customer?), need (what does he need and want, and how much?), and purchasing behaviour (who is the customer and what is his buying process?). You will wish to develop a segmentation approach which suits the needs of your directorate; the following examples should help.

Segmenting patients

- referring practice
- age
- gender
- socio-economic group
- condition
- diagnosis (HRG)
- procedure (OPCS-4).

Segmenting GPs

- practice location
- fundholding/non-fundholding
- number of GPs in practice
- practice budget
- number of referrals from practice.

It is likely that, if you undertake a thorough market segmentation, you will identify a large number of market segments. The next stage must therefore be to decide which of these market segments have the highest priority; the reality of life in a clinical directorate means that these are likely to be patients (grouped, perhaps, by HRG), commissioners, GPs, and other hospital directorates and departments, but may also include, in a teaching hospital, for instance, students, the University School of Medicine, referring hospitals, and commissions. Decisions on priorities will be based on a combination of financial necessity, management pressure, political guidance, and the importance to you of the service provided by your internal customers, and they will be different for each directorate.

Market research

So you have decided which of these many market segments or customer groups is the most important. How can you ensure that you provide the service necessary to ensure customer satisfaction and, for internal customers, that you provide each other with the service needed to support the effective delivery of patient care? You must establish the needs and expectations of customers in each segment – and by far the best way is to do some market research. Your commissioners' contracts will certainly be based on some market research, although market research into the views of the general public about the priorities for health care spending is notoriously difficult and unreliable. This topic is really the province of health economists, so we will not cover it here. Carrying out research into the needs of the local GP population may be difficult but it is undoubtedly worthwhile. The most effective approach consists of two stages.

1 Use an experienced market researcher to recruit a selection of your GPs to a focus group to elicit their views about the range of services they would like to see, and then to report back to you. It is preferable to use a third party facilitator as this will protect you from the possibility of becoming involved in a slanging match with GPs who have axes to grind.

2 Get the market researcher to compile a concise questionnaire which you can circulate to all your GPs so that you can establish their needs and priorities as a group. You will wish to include some demographic questions to enable you to distinguish between, for instance, the needs of large and small practices or between the needs of inner city and rural practices.

Researching the needs and expectations of your colleagues in other directorates and departments may also be difficult to organize but it is always worth meeting them to have the discussion. Even if you have been providing or receiving a satisfactory service for years, it may well be that there are changes afoot which will change what your customers want from you or how they provide a service to you.

Marketing mix

There is a widely accepted model of the components of a product or service which is relevant here. It is colloquially known as the '4Ps' model, and is shown in Box 5.4.

Box 5.4: Marketing mix – '4Ps' model

Product/service	The actual product or service which is being delivered, such as those listed in Box 5.5
Promotion	The information provided to customers about the service, its availability, price, target market, etc.
Distribution channel ('place')	The means by which the service is delivered to the consumer; in the case of a service this includes the people who provide the service
Price	The price of the service or, in the case of an internal customer, the cost to him in terms of time, etc.

So, in order for a customer to be able to avail himself of the service, all the other parts of the marketing mix must be in place too. You must be providing him with information about the service, there must be a clear route for him to gain access, and it must be clear to him what costs he is going to incur.

It is clear that different groups of customers will need you to provide different services, or be looking for different things in the same service. For instance, for an initial outpatient appointment:

- a GP fundholder may require you to provide the consultation within two weeks of his request at a given cost

- a non-fundholding GP may require the same service but will have no direct concern with cost

- the patient may expect not to have to wait more than half an hour after the time of his appointment and to be kindly and courteously treated

- the ambulance service may expect the patient to have completed the consultation by the time agreed

- the outpatients department may expect you to have completed the consultation within the time allowed so that other patients do not have to wait too long for their consultations.

As is now well understood in most NHS Trusts, a GP's view of the service provided by a hospital is that it consists of everything which happens to the patient during his or her stay in hospital (Box 5.5). This set of activities for a given service constitutes the 'product' part of the marketing mix.

Box 5.5: A GP's view of an inpatient stay

Admission
Diagnosis
Nursing care
Procedures
Drugs and dressings
Recovery
Therapy
Discharge
Discharge summary

Promotion is becoming an increasingly important dimension of a Trust's activities, not least because of the competitive environment in which Trusts now operate. Almost every Trust has its prospectus, which typically sets out the services provided, the facilities used to provide them, and the staff who provide them. If the prospectus is well designed, it will be found on the bookshelf of every GP in the catchment area. It is therefore in your interest to ensure that it meets the needs of GPs in your area and that your directorate is properly represented. But is that enough? One-to-one communication is time-consuming but if you are able to spend the time talking to your GP population you can expand on the information contained in the Trust prospectus and deal with queries about your service offering on the spot. GP receptions are sometimes used for this purpose but their effectiveness is limited by the fact that only sympathetic GPs bother to attend. It may therefore be worth investing the time to visit practices to talk about the services you offer.

A distribution channel, or 'place' as it is known in the '4Ps' model, is the set of systems, procedures, and people which enables a customer to ask for a service to be provided and enables you to provide it. Taking the GP example again, the GP sends referrals, patients, and money to you, and in return you provide a service. The distribution channel in this case consists of the means of transferring information, money, and patients between the GP and your directorate; it therefore includes telecommunications, the postal service, and the ambulance service, as well as infrastructures in the GP surgery and your Trust.

The meaning of 'price' appears self-evident except that, from the customer's point of view, it includes not only what they pay you, but all the other costs they incur as well. This may include such things as the cost of time wasted dealing with patients who have to wait for their appointments and time spent on the telephone negotiating for a bed.

The GP's measure of a quality service is that every aspect of the patient's visit to hospital is of high quality, and it is therefore in the clinical director's interest to ensure that every department in the hospital does its job well. This includes all the clinical departments but also includes support departments such as medical records, catering, and estates, and it is most unwise for the clinical director to take a parochial view of what happens in his directorate.

An understanding of your markets is a key prerequisite to developing a business strategy, since your directorate's *raison d'être* is the satisfaction of the needs of its external and internal customers. We shall now discuss how to use this and other information to develop your strategic plan.

Strategic planning process

There are as many ways of developing a strategic plan as there are people doing it, and there is considerable scope for the exercise of personal preference. However, there are key stages which have to be undertaken if the strategic plan is to be a sound one, and they are shown in Figure 5.1. They are:

- assessing the strengths and weaknesses of your directorate and the favourable and/or unfavourable impacts which changes in the external environment might have on your eventual strategies

- agreeing your directorate's aspirations

- stating assumptions: no matter how careful your analysis, you sometimes have to make assumptions about how the environment is going to behave and it is important to state them

- deciding what you are setting out to achieve

- planning how you are going to achieve those things

- deciding who is going to do what, by when, and with what resources.

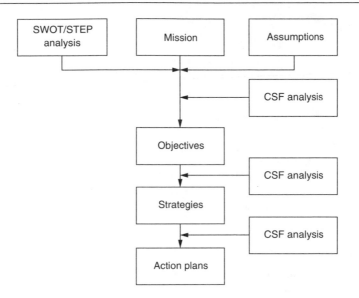

Figure 5.1: Strategic planning process.

Assumptions

The authors have seen several recent cases where directorates in a Trust have based their strategic plans on different, even conflicting assumptions; e.g. the directorate including obstetrics assumed that they would experience a 20 per cent loss of maternity cases to a nearby Trust whereas that responsible for ultrasound assumed no reduction in cases. Had this not been spotted during the review process, there would have been a significant, and costly, over-provision of ultrasound facilities. It is inevitable that, due to their different points of view and sources of information, directorates will make different assumptions. The only way of correcting this is to:

- state assumptions clearly in the strategic plan

- highlight in the plan situations where planned activity is based on assumptions

- circulate these assumptions to other directorates for comment

- be prepared to revise these assumptions after discussion with other directorates affected.

It is critically important that everyone works to the same assumptions; where there are assumptions, such as those about contracted activity levels, which affect several directorates, it is helpful for the Trust senior management to take the lead in stating them at the beginning of the strategic planning round.

Mission statement

> You got to have a dream,
> If you don't have a dream,
> How you gonna have a dream come true?
>
> Rodgers and Hammerstein,
> 'South Pacific', 1949

A mission statement is a statement of your directorate's aspirations and, as such, is usually focused on a point some years in the future. It summarizes and encapsulates your long-term goals, your values and norms, or what you desire them to be, and its development must involve all directorate managers and its senior staff – all the people who might reasonably claim to be the guardians of what you stand for. A mission statement:

- describes your aspirations

- sets out your view of the future

- motivates you and your staff

- ensures you are all striving for the same things.

For example: 'We strive to provide a comprehensive cancer care service offering the best in clinical practice, to minimize fear and pain, and offer our patients a personal service which preserves dignity and confidentiality' and 'Our mission is to become an international centre of excellence in our discipline through practice, teaching, and research'.

The authors often come across statements which proclaim not the aspirations of the directorate but what it currently stands for; this is a perfectly valid and useful statement, which we prefer to call the rôle of the directorate, but it is not a mission statement. A rôle statement covers:

- what justifies your existence

- what people know you for

- how you describe what you do

- and gives a sense of identity to everyone in the directorate.

For example: 'The pathology department provides high quality services to hospital and primary health care customers in an efficient and timely way' and 'The physiotherapy department provides a prompt, high quality service to meet the identified needs of patients at the ABC NHS Trust'.

SWOT analysis and STEP analysis

Perhaps the simplest, most commonly used, and commonly abused, forms of strategic analysis are STEP analysis and SWOT analysis. They are, respectively, an analysis of the impact on an organization of the Sociological, Technological, Economic, and Political dimensions of its environment and an analysis of its Strengths, Weaknesses, Opportunities, and Threats. What is the point of these analyses? STEP analysis is a way of analysing your external environment in order to spot those current or future changes which may have an effect on what you choose to do, or on your chances of success in achieving what you choose to do. SWOT analysis helps you to analyse your own organization and the impact on it of changes in the environment.

A *strength* is a unique asset or competence, or an asset or competence that is better than your competitors' or, perhaps, something in which you have achieved standards of best practice.

A *weakness* is where you are less well equipped or skilled than your competitors or where you are some way from achieving standards of best practice.

An *opportunity* is something which you have the choice to do, or may have the choice to do, if you have the right resources and choose to deploy them as appropriate; the implication is that this course of action will necessitate the withdrawal of those resources from where they are currently deployed (i.e. there is an opportunity cost).

A *threat* is something which confronts you, or may confront you, which may prevent or hinder your achievement of your goals; in order to deal with this threat you may have to divert resources from where you had planned to deploy them.

By and large, strengths and weaknesses are internal and opportunities and threats are external; there is thus a degree of redundancy in that both techniques involve some environmental analysis – hence the authors have developed a form of SWOT analysis which subsumes STEP analysis, with a consequent saving in time and improvement in consistency.

The preferred approach to SWOT analysis is to run a workshop with a small, cross-disciplinary group with relevant knowledge and experience; perhaps the directorate management team augmented with a few representatives of those directorates and departments with whom you work most closely. This ensures that you canvass a variety of opinions and reach a balanced conclusion; our experience is that the workshop also helps members of the group to understand each other's points of view. If you are unable to run a workshop, desk analysis is a good second best as long as you give others the opportunity of commenting on what you have done. But before you start, what do you mean by 'strengths', 'weaknesses', 'opportunities', and 'threats' respectively?

The first stage in doing a SWOT analysis is to state the objective of your analysis clearly and unambiguously. If you fail to do this, you will have no basis for deciding whether any claimed strength, weakness, opportunity, or threat is relevant or important. For example, a directorate responsible for obstetrics might set an objective 'To assess the directorate's SWOTs with a view to defending its contracts for obstetric services against competition from XYZ NHS

Trust'. From this it will be evident that it will often be necessary to do more than one SWOT analysis, though often you will be able to re-visit one you have done before.

The next stage is to brainstorm potential SWOTs; even when you have set a clear objective this is difficult unless the discussion has some better focus. Our approach is to carry out a series of 'mini-SWOT' analyses, each focusing on a particular aspect of the organization or its environment. A list of suitable topics is shown in Box 5.6; this list may be modified to suit your own needs; for instance, your directorate may not be dependent on 'raw materials' but may be very technologically advanced; under such circumstance you might give the 'raw materials' mini-SWOT only a cursory glance but break the 'technology' mini-SWOT into 'pharmaceuticals', 'equipment', and 'procedures'. The brain storming process is likely to highlight a number of potential SWOTs for each mini-SWOT analysis, and it is important to retain in the analysis only those which will make some contribution to your strategic planning. There are several tests you can apply:

- is it relevant?

- is it unique to you?

- if it's not unique to you, is it the same for you as it is for the Trust next door?

- if so, is it more or less true for you than it is for your competitors?

- is it important?

Only SWOTs which pass all these tests should be kept; you should note that, for instance, an apparent strength is neutral if all your potential competitors are just as strong.

The most usual way of presenting the results of SWOT analysis is to use a chart like that in Figure 5.2. Another point to note is that it is not uncommon for a particular factor to appear in more than one quadrant. For instance, difficulty in recruiting skilled staff may be a strength if you have good staff and are good at keeping them because it will make it difficult for others to recruit. However, if you have good staff and can't keep them, or if you have poor staff, it will be a threat to you.

By the time you have worked through 20 or 30 analyses, you will discover that some SWOTs come up time and again in different analyses; this is an indication that they are important, though not the only indication; you will certainly have developed some views about which SWOTs are important and which are not. However, you will have identified a large number of factors, far too many to be useful in any subsequent planning activity, so the next stage is to consolidate all these mini-SWOT analyses into a single overall analysis containing the most important five each of strengths, weaknesses, opportunities, and threats.

Box 5.6: SWOT analysis topics

finance: availability of funds
technology: changes in equipment, processes, and procedures
supra-national: e.g. European Union, ex-Eastern bloc, UN, etc.
legislation/regulation: current and pending

cultural: ethnic minorities, changes in 'normal' behaviour, drug use
competitors: other Trusts, private sector, primary sector
professional organizations: attitudes to management and changing rôles of clinicians
customers/clients: GPs (fundholding and non-fundholding), commissioners, health insurance companies, etc.
distributors: voluntary bodies

corporate infrastructure: directorate structure, buildings and facilities, telecommunications, transport
financial management: availability and quality, flexibility, innovation
technology development: R&D, support from biotechnology
inbound logistics: ambulance Trusts, admissions procedures, outpatients procedures
marketing: knowledge of requirements of Commissioners, GPs and other purchasers and ability to educate and promote to them
outbound logistics: discharge procedures, ambulance Trusts, outpatients procedures

labour market: need, availability of staff
raw materials: changes in prices, availability, quality
politics: new policies, changes in Government, openness to influence
social: e.g. greying population, other demographic shifts
economics: local, national and supra-national economic trends
unions: attitudes to changing labour practices, IPR etc.
facilitators: management consultants, advisory bodies, quangos
suppliers: pharmaceuticals, equipment, catering, bank staff, etc.

collaborators: private investors in infrastructure development, pharmaceutical companies
corporate and marketing strategy: clarity of vision, staff commitment, empathy with directorate strategy
HR management: availability and quality, flexibility, innovation
procurement: negotiating skills, knowledge of supply market place
operations: general day-to-day management capability

sales: ability to identify and negotiate contracts and to identify new sources of client revenue
after sales service: complaints procedures, follow-up and domiciliary services

Strengths	Weaknesses
Opportunities	Threats

Figure 5.2: Presenting SWOT analysis.

Critical Success Factors analysis

It is usually taken for granted that you wish to be successful in your chosen job or profession and the same is true of your directorate or department; however, this begs the question of what you mean by success. In a corporate environment you usually mean the achievement of some goal which you have set yourself and/or agreed with your peers or managers; success might therefore be defined as the achievement of your mission. Critical Success Factors (CSF) analysis is a way of working out what you need to do to be successful by whatever measure you have chosen. Critical Success Factors are those tasks which are necessary and sufficient for success; if you complete them all you will succeed but if you don't complete one of them you will fail. The research carried out by Professor Jack Rockart, a distinguished American academic who developed the technique, reveals that, for any success measure, there are between five and seven CSFs; since CSFs are necessary and sufficient they are all equally important.[2] Rockart developed a rigorous technique for identifying CSFs which is beyond the scope of this book; however, the authors' experience indicates that a directorate management team workshop will have little difficulty in agreeing which of the many tasks it could carry out are, in fact, critical. Interestingly, some of Rockart's research was carried out in the US health care industry; the CSFs identified for a US government hospital are shown in Box 5.7.

Box 5.7: CSFs for a US hospital

Hospital information system
Resource allocation
External relationships
Commitment of hospital directors
Management capability
Relationship with US Department
Budgetary constraints

In the current UK environment, one CSF which is almost universal is meeting Patient's Charter standards and any other measures which HM Government may put in place from time to time. However, as illustrated vividly by Patient's Charter standards, merely defining your CSFs does not ensure that you achieve them. You must put an action plan in place (see below), monitor that action plan, and take corrective action if it seems that the achievement of one of your CSFs is in doubt. Figure 5.1 includes three boxes marked 'CSF analysis'. As will be explained later, it is the CSF analysis process, rather than its outputs, which are valuable; nevertheless, some strategic planners like to see the outputs included as appendices to the strategic plan.

Objectives

An objective states a commitment to achieve a significant desired outcome. It must be SMARTO: Specific, Measurable, Agreed/achievable, Realistic, Timed, and Owned. Objectives are a very important part of the strategic planning process because they are the point at which the organization's and the individual's interests converge. In Chapter 2 we discussed objectives in the context of individual performance target setting and appraisal, and we are talking about the same objectives. The members of the directorate management team between them own the directorate's objectives; in order to ensure the achievement of these objectives, it is likely that each member of the team will need to devolve parts of each objective to members of the directorate.

Objectives derive from several sources; they may do any of the things shown in Box 5.8. The last objective in Box 5.8 is an example of one which fails the SMARTO test; you have no alternative but to regard Patient's Charter targets as objectives, even though they are imposed, they may not be achievable and you may regard them as inappropriate.

Objectives are not the same as CSFs; they will often be prioritized and, except for objectives which derive from CSFs, not completing them will not constitute failure *per se*. But ensure that, whatever else you do, you achieve the CSFs.

Box 5.8: Types of objective, with examples

Support the achievement of a CSF	To develop an effective channel of communications with fundholding GPs by the end of March 1997
Exploit a strength	To increase ECRs to your MRI scanner by 10 per cent this year
Correct a weakness	To ensure that we have full paediatric nursing cover for SCBU by the end of December this year
Exploit an opportunity	To secure Regional funds to update your radiotherapy facilities by the end of next year
Pre-empt a threat	To ensure that your relationships with GP fundholders are such that we experience no loss of business to XYZ hospital's new obstetrics wing
Result from external target-setting	To ensure that we meet all your Patient's Charter targets by the end of this year

Strategies

The word strategy is widely misused by managers, and not only in the NHS. What we mean by a strategy is the programme of activities which you have to put in place to ensure the achievement of an objective. In order to have a strategy you need to know your starting point, as given by your SWOT analysis, and where you want to arrive, your objective. A strategy is descriptive: it describes how you are going to achieve the objective, and when, but not in great detail; this is the job of an action plan. Sometimes, as in building a new hospital, the strategy is simple but the action plan is so complex that a project management team is appointed to draw up, agree, and implement the action plan. You may use the CSF process to help you derive your strategies from your objectives by asking yourselves, for each objective, what activities you must carry out in order to ensure the success of that objective. Your strategy will consist only of those activities which are necessary and sufficient for success, a vital requirement in a severely resource-limited world. See Box 5.9 for an example strategy.

Quite often, you discover that the relationship between objectives and strategies is not one-to-one; some strategies support more than one objective, and some objectives need more than one strategy. Under such circumstances it is possible to omit something important or, more often, do more than is necessary. It is commonplace for organizations, whether companies or departments, to have a strategy in each of several key areas, so that each strategy contributes to the achievement of several

---

Box 5.9: Example strategy

Our strategy is

To promote our services to our commissioners and GP fundholders so that we establish a steady, reliable revenue stream.

To ensure that we continue to provide a high-quality, cost effective service to our commissioners and GP fundholders.

To secure funding for the new wing by the end of 1996, with a view to completion by mid-1998.

To plan the transfer of services to the new wing during 1998–1999, releasing the old building for re-development.

To develop positive relationships with adjacent Trusts with a view to avoiding damaging and pointless competition.

---

objectives. Common composite strategies are those for the principal corporate resources of finance, information, human resources, services, and land and buildings. It is also common to have some strategies, such as training and marketing, at a lower level.

There is a simple way of ensuring that between them the strategies will result in the achievement of the objectives. This makes use of the matrix in Figure 5.3. The approach is to list your objectives and strategies along the two dimensions of the matrix and then use a simple scoring method (e.g. 0, 1, 2, 3, or blank, L, M, H) to indicate the level of support given by each strategy to the achievement of each objective. It will soon become apparent that some objectives have more strategic support than they need, and some very little. Under these circumstances should you

- add, modify or drop a strategy?
- add, modify or drop an objective?

so that the objectives are achieved in the most effective way. The final question must always be to ask yourselves if you have the resources to put these strategies into effect. Sometimes management teams are guilty of group-think and set themselves objectives that they cannot possibly achieve, particularly in the context of continuing to provide patient care. It is better to modify your objectives at the beginning of the year than to have to do so, sometimes very visibly, towards the end of the year when the pressure is on.

Action plans

When you have finalized your strategies, and are happy that you have the resources to complete them, the last step in the planning process is to develop an

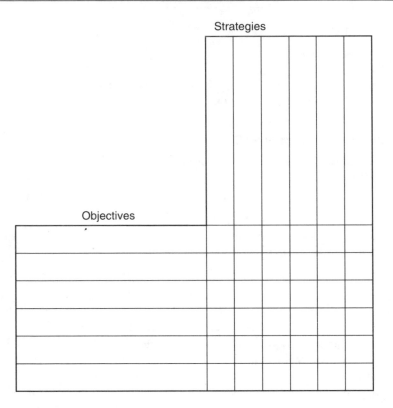

Figure 5.3: Objectives/strategies matrix.

action plan (Figure 5.4). Decades of experience show that, unless organizational commitments are turned into individual responsibilities, little or nothing will happen. The point of an action plan, then, is that every strategy is broken into its component parts and a named individual takes responsibility for each part. They will be unwilling to do this unless the organization commits to them the resources and authority necessary to take the requisite action, so action planning can be a time-consuming and difficult exercise.

Yet again, you may use the CSF process for each strategy, by asking yourselves what actions you must carry out in order to ensure the achievement of that strategy, again with the beneficial effect that you include in your action plan only those actions which are necessary and sufficient for the success of the strategy. What commonly emerges at this point is that, despite the best endeavours of everyone in the management team to ensure that there are enough resources to put a strategy into effect, the people being asked to do so are unable to satisfy themselves that this is the case. Under such circumstances, as shown in Figure 5.5,

Action	Who	By when	Review date	Resources

Figure 5.4: Action plan format.

you have no alternative but to revise your strategies; this in turn may lead to a re-evaluation of objectives and, exceptionally, may suggest that the mission statement is asking too much of the organization.

Contingency plans

Despite the care you have put into stating your assumptions, your evaluation of the external environment, and the development of your mission, objectives,

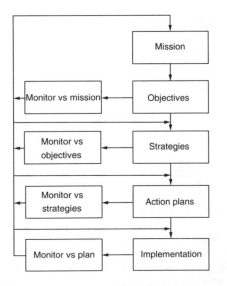

Figure 5.5: Strategic planning process, with feedback loops.

strategies, and action plans (Box 5.10), things will go wrong. In Chapter 6 we talk about assessing and managing risk but here we shall briefly discuss contingency planning. The process is a simple one: you must review what can go wrong with your strategies, and then decide what you will do if it does. Contingency plans should have to deal only with external factors, since your knowledge of your own resources should preclude you committing yourselves to strategies which won't work. A contingency plan is really an alternative strategy, and you may well develop one as a by-product of strategy generation. The simplest approach is:

- to look at each of your assumptions, and ask what you will do if that assumption proves incorrect; this may lead to a change in an objective, or to a change in the strategy which supports that objective

- to look at the threats in your SWOT analysis, and ask how you will cope if that threat becomes a reality; this is likely to mean that you will have to switch resources from one strategy to another, which will force you to modify a strategy and may force you to change an objective

- to look at the opportunities in your SWOT analysis, and ask what you will do if you decide that you must capitalize on that opportunity, which will have the same effects as a threat.

Of course, contingency planning won't prevent the unexpected but it will give you some hope of being able to cope with it without the whole directorate being plunged into confusion.

Box 5.10: Typical strategic plan contents

rôle
mission
SWOT analysis
objectives
strategies

References

1 Taylor B. (1984) Strategic planning: which style do you need? *Long Range Planning*. 17(3): 51–62.
2 Rockart J. (1979) Chief executives define their own data needs. *Harvard Business Review*. 57(2): 81–93.

Service delivery planning

Noel Austin

In the previous chapter we discussed strategic planning, which is about changing what we do. However, for many people in the NHS, life is about doing their best to treat patients and maintain the status quo in a hostile and unpredictable environment. It is a popular fiction that, under such circumstances, it is impossible to plan. The purpose of this chapter is to show you that this is not the case by providing you with a set of tools with which you can plan service delivery.

Although this chapter has been written from the viewpoint of someone in a mainstream medical or surgical directorate, all the techniques are easily adapted to suit the needs of a support directorate or department such as radiology, pathology, physiotherapy, or pharmacy.

The first point to make is that service planning is not about planning how to treat individual patients, which is outside the scope of this volume. Its purpose is to assess what resources you need to treat the mix of patients who are likely to be referred to you over the planning period, in such a way that you minimize the likelihood of being under- or over-resourced. Hence the patterns of treatment you give to different types of patient is of great interest to you; if you know what resources you need to treat each type of patient, and you have some idea of what case mix will be referred to you, you have some hope of being able to muster the total resources needed to provide all your patients with a quality service or, at the very worst, to assess the impact of a resource shortfall.

The service planning process consists of a number of stages, each of which may undergo a number of iterations, certainly every year but often more frequently. As we indicated in Chapter 5, it is necessary to make assumptions and, because you live in a changing world, these assumptions will often be wrong. As soon as you spot that one of your assumptions is wrong, you must consider whether you should re-visit your plan to assess the impact.

One of the biggest challenges of the service planning process is that, in your service plans, you must take account of the changes envisaged in your strategic plans and of the resources needed to implement them. It is also easy in strategic planning to become over-ambitious and to commit yourself to changes which you cannot possibly resource. So, in developing your service plans, you must take account of the strategic action plans to which you have committed yourself.

Service planning approach

Perhaps the first point to address is 'What is meant by a service?'. In the NHS of today, you must define your services in terms of how commissioners or GP fundholders wish to contract for or purchase them. In other words, a service is likely to consist of everything that happens to a patient during a stay in hospital, from admission, clerking by the house officer, all consultant involvement, diagnostic tests, procedures, drugs, therapies, social work involvement, and discharge, perhaps even including follow-up outpatients appointments and any subsequent re-admissions. In other words, codes currently used by doctors to describe patient diagnoses or procedures, such as Read codes, ICD-9, or OPCS-4, are unlikely to be adequate. The most promising candidate appears to be the newly defined Healthcare Resource Groups (HRGs), which are superior to Diagnostic Resource Groups (DRGs) in that an individual HRG covers only one diagnosis. DRGs, which were developed for the US insurance industry, often cover unrelated conditions with similar costs – fine for insurers but useless for service planning.

A typical clinical directorate provides a wide range of services. Some are in constant demand, or have a clear seasonal pattern, and some are requested infrequently or on an *ad hoc* basis. If your directorate management team is not to be buried under a mass of data it should concentrate its attention on planning those services which constitute the majority of the directorate's workload, on the basis that if it can plan, say, 80 per cent of its work, managers will have more time to spend on managing the less predictable 20 per cent. The preferred approach is therefore to plan the directorate's key services which are, say, those most frequently requested services which, together, consume 80 per cent of the directorate's resources.

So how can you establish which are your key services? This depends on the quality of management information available to you. If you are fortunate enough to work in a Trust where resource management systems have been fully implemented (see Chapter 8), it may be possible to frame a request such that you can obtain a list of your services in decreasing order of cost or resource utilization. If your Trust does not have a fully implemented resource management system, the process will be more protracted. In such a situation the following approach can be used – it requires an investment of time by clinical staff but it generates sound service delivery plans.

- Select a sample of patients, such as all those patients discharged from the directorate over a three-month period.

- Using discharge summaries, allocate each patient episode to a resource category, such as an HRG.

- Produce a summary sheet for each episode, on which you record the number of days spent in hospital during that episode.

- Batch the summary sheets by resource category and calculate the total bed-days occupied by patients in each batch.

- Sort the batches into descending order of number of days of bed occupancy and select those which together constitute, say, 80 per cent of utilized bed-days; these are your key services.

You may reasonably argue that the number of bed-days is a crude measure of resource utilization but, in the absence of information systems, it may be the only easily accessible measure. Your list of key services may be as few as 15–20 or as many as 60; in a directorate of general medicine where this process was used, the key services were:

- diabetes
- myocardial infarction
- cardiac failure
- CVA
- chest infection
- angina
- neoplastic disease
- non-cardiac chest pain
- TIA
- GI bleeding
- arrhythmia
- epilepsy
- alcoholism
- DVT
- urinary infection
- gastro-enteritis
- headache
- peptic ulcer
- syncope
- viral illness.

Retain the summary sheets for patient episodes in those key services, and collect detailed information about all clinical interventions in each patient episode, as indicated in Table 6.1.

Table 6.1: Resource data for clinical interventions

Who is involved?	Activities (units)	Information sources
House officers	Clerking (hours)	Patient notes
Consultant physicians and registrars	Ward rounds and discharge summaries (hours)	Patient notes
Consultant surgeons and registrars	Ward rounds, procedures, and discharge summaries (hours)	Patient notes, theatre records
Anaesthetists	Pre-operative and post-operative visits, procedures (hours)	Patient notes, theatre records
Theatres	Theatre time (hours)	Theatre records
Nurses	Clinical interventions (hours)	Care plans, patient notes
Therapists	Clinical interventions (hours)	Patient records, therapy records
Pharmacy	Drugs and chemotherapy (doses), clinical pharmacy (hours)	Patient notes, pharmacy records
Radiology	Radiography and radiotherapy (Körner units), reporting (hours)	Patient notes, radiology records
Pathology	Tests (Welcan units), reporting and clinical pathology (hours)	Patient notes, pathology records
Social workers	Discharge planning (hours)	Patient records, social work notes

This data collection provides you with a record of the resources used in caring for each patient in your sample; it is now a simple matter to calculate the average length of stay and average pattern of care for patients in each of your key services. However, to enable the patient to stay in hospital a variety of other resources are used, including housekeeping, portering and catering, and a range of patient related tasks carried out by nurses and care assistants but which do not constitute clinical interventions. It is probably easiest to regard these as a form of directorate overhead, with the resources averaged across occupied bed-days.

You will note that what you have done here is to use a sample of past activity data to provide an estimate of future resource usage. In this way, you took account of the resources used in treating complications and secondary diagnoses, and in enabling the patient to stay in hospital, which you could not have done if you had based your estimates on protocols.

Service description

A service description (SD) is a way of pulling together all the information you have about the ways in which you provide service and using these:

- to develop your own resource plans
- to negotiate with your suppliers about the provision of their resources
- to negotiate with commissioners and GP fundholders in full knowledge of your own service costs.

In some ways a SD is similar to a care profile except that it includes information about your customers, their use of your services, and the costs you incur in providing them. In the general case a SD will consist of the items set out in Box 6.1. Figure 6.1 to Figure 6.4 provide an example of this approach in practice. You may find it helpful to define a service called a 'standard bed-day' as a repository for all the direct costs incurred in caring for a patient which were not the result of clinical interventions. The elements might include:

- ward based medical care
- housekeeping
- catering
- portering
- indirect nursing care (e.g. care planning, shift hand-over meetings)
- care assistants
- nursing management and supervision.

In each case, you average the total cost for the ward across the number of occupied bed-days; you may choose to ignore the minor variations in cost-per-patient due to such factors as diet meals and differing demands on the services of care assistants. You may find yourself obliged to average some other costs in the same way if appropriate information systems are not available. This may require an uncomfortable compromise but service planning, like politics, is the art of the possible (Box 6.2).

Service requirements

It can be seen that, in the process of developing SDs, you have calculated the demands you intend to make on each of your resource suppliers, such as radiology and pathology, for each of the services they provide. Given that you know or are able to estimate your case mix, you can then calculate the total demand you intend to make for each service supplied; see examples in Figures 6.5–6.6.

Box 6.1: Contents of typical service description

Name	Brief name by which the service is commonly known. May also include code, such as HRG, particularly if IT systems in use
Description	Brief description which indicates the scope of the service and the major investigations and treatments which comprise it
Constraints	Limits on number of cases at any one time, or per time period. This may be based on available beds, people, or some technical resource
Future trends	An indication of any trends, such as new drugs or procedures which may change the way in which this service is delivered, which may increase demand, or which may make it redundant
Competition	Other Trusts or private hospitals which may compete with you in offering this service
Current customers	Commissioners or GP fundholders who currently obtain this purchasers' service from you
Potential customers	Commissioners or GP fundholders whom you might be able to persuade to obtain this service from you
Volumes	Estimated numbers of referrals from current and potential purchasers
Price	The price which each current and potential purchaser is prepared to pay for this service (this may be expressed in terms of block, cost and volume or cost per case contract prices)
Length of stay	Average number of bed-days occupied by patients referred to this service
For each type of clinical intervention	Type of intervention Number of interventions of this type Number of units of resource Unit cost per unit Total cost per type of intervention
Cost per case	Total cost for all interventions

Specialty	General medicine	**ID**	GM1
Service name	Diabetes	**ID**	GM001

Brief description
As a temporary measure this service includes both short-stay patients being re-balanced and long-term patients with complications.

Constraints
Nursing expertise in treating and counselling diabetic patients and their relatives is currently concentrated on Ward 23.

Future trends

Competition
Diabetic patients are treated in most nearby acute hospitals but the majority of diabetic patients enter the hospital as emergency admissions.

Prepared by	Noel Austin	**Version no**	0.3
Authorized by	P M Blackmore	**Date**	21-Apr-97

Figure 6.1: Service description: overview.

| Specialty | General medicine | | | | ID | GM1 |

Specialty General medicine   **ID** GM1

Service name Diabetes   **ID** GM001

Current market

Purchaser ID	Purchaser	Annual volume	Price	Annual revenue
	Midshire Health Authority	320		
	Smith, Smith & Cooper	25		
			345		

Potential market

Purchaser ID	Purchaser	Annual volume	Price	Annual revenue
	Patel & Johnson	20		
			20		

Prepared by Noel Austin   **Version no** 0.3

Authorized by P M Blackmore   **Date** 21-Apr-97

Figure 6.2: Service description: markets

| Specialty | General medicine | | ID | GM1 |
| Service name | Diabetes | | ID | GM001 |

Event ID	Description	Number	Unit cost	Total cost
	General medicine standard bed day	17.90		
	Service related patient care hours	74.05		
	Based on GRASP patient care hours and assuming a utilization rate of 110%.			
	Radiology: chest X-ray	1.00		
	Haematology: FBC	1.00		
	Haematology: B12	1.00		
	Haematology: folate	1.00		
	Haematology: iron	1.00		
	Haematology: clotting test	5.00		
	Biochemistry: U+E	2.00		
	Biochemistry: profile	2.00		
	Biochemistry: TFT	1.00		
	Biochemistry: HbA	1.00		
	Cardiology: ECG	1.00		
	No reliable analysis of pharmacy costs is yet available, so all hospital pharmacy and drug costs are included in the general medicine standard bed-day cost.			

| Prepared by | Noel Austin | | Version no | 0.3 |
| Authorized by | P M Blackmore | | Date | 21-Apr-97 |

Figure 6.3: Service description: care profile.

Specialty	General medicine		ID	GM1

Service name	Diabetes		ID	GM001

Cost summary

Supplier ID	Supplier	
RA1	Radiology	
PA1	Diagnostic haematology	
PA2	Medical biochemistry	
CA1	Cardiology	

Cost per case

Notes

Prepared by	Noel Austin		Version no	0.3

Authorized by	P M Blackmore		Date	21-Apr-97

Figure 6.4: Service description: cost summary.

Box 6.2: Typical service plan contents

Clients
Services provided
Contractual basis
Resources
Policy statements
Development plans
Budgets
Management arrangements

These service requirements then form the basis of the commitments you need to seek from your suppliers for their services. The best way of negotiating these commitments, whilst providing a basis for continual monitoring of service quality and volume, is to use Service Level Agreements.

Service Level Agreements

A Service Level Agreement (SLA), sometimes known as a Service Agreement, is a form of internal contract between the user of a resource, such as a directorate or specialty, and its provider. Typical SLAs cover the provision of x-rays, pathology tests, and therapeutic interventions, but can also cover such things as bed swapping between directorates and the provision of services by support functions such as finance, personnel, and information. A SLA provides the customer with guarantees of service provision and provides the supplier with a demand forecast. Many people, including the authors, argue that there is no reason why a SLA should make any reference to money; there seems little point in shuffling money between Directorates unless the process adds value. However, the benefit of an SLA is that both sides have a clear statement of what each expects from the other and an agreed basis for monitoring service provision (Box 6.3).

Of course, SLAs are not worth the paper they are written on unless they are supported by information systems which report recent performance against the standards set in the SLA. This applies both to suppliers and ourselves – quality aware managers know before their customers when there has been a problem, and have already decided what to do about it. For instance, if radiology anticipates problems in supporting endoscopy services because of staff shortages, or if general medicine expects a reduction in referrals requiring endoscopic examination, it is important that they tell each other as soon as possible. This enables both parties to optimize resource utilization.

| | | Specialty | General medicine | | ID | GM1 |

	Specialty	General medicine			ID	GM1
	Supplier	Diabetes			ID	GM001
	Service	Full blood count			ID	PA101

Our service ID	Our service name	Annual demand	Usage per service	Total required
GM001	Diabetes	320	1.00	320
GM002	Myocardial infarction	460	1.00	460
GM003	Cardiac failure	210	1.00	210
GM004	CVA	330	1.00	330
GM005	Chest infection	270	2.00	540
GM006	Angina	380	1.00	380
GM007	Neoplastic disease	140	2.00	280
GM008	Non-cardiac chest pain	410	1.00	410
GM009	TIA	160	1.00	160
GM010	GI bleeding	270	3.00	810
GM011	Arrhythmia	140	1.00	140
GM012	Epilepsy	190	1.00	190
GM013	Alcoholism	80	2.00	160
GM014	DVT	130	1.00	130
GM015	Urinary infection	100	2.00	200
GM016	Gastroenteritis	80	2.00	160
GM017	Headache	100	1.00	100
GM018	Peptic ulcer	80	1.00	80
GM019	Syncope	80	1.00	80
GM020	Viral illness	100	1.00	100
	Other inpatient	870	1.00	870
	Outpatient: first appointment	5000	0.30	1500
	Outpatient: follow-up	20 000	0.10	2000
				9610

| Prepared by | Noel Austin | | Version no | 0.4 |
| Authorized by | P M Blackmore/R K Smith | | Date | 25-May-97 |

Figure 6.5: Service requirement: resource requirement worksheet: FBC.

Specialty	General medicine		ID	GM1
Supplier	General medicine		ID	GM1
Service	Nursing care		ID	GM098

Our service ID	Our service name	Annual demand	Usage per service	Total required
GM001	Diabetes	320	72.20	23 104
GM002	Myocardial infarction	460	19.17	8818
GM003	Cardiac failure	210	42.13	8847
GM004	CVA	330	33.87	11 177
GM005	Chest infection	270	25.47	6877
GM006	Angina	380	26.33	10 005
GM007	Neoplastic disease	140	38.10	5334
GM008	Non-cardiac chest pain	410	6.70	2747
GM009	TIA	160	17.20	2752
GM010	GI bleeding	270	13.20	3564
GM011	Arrhythmia	140	25.67	3594
GM012	Epilepsy	190	16.60	3154
GM013	Alcoholism	80	28.33	2266
GM014	DVT	130	19.80	2574
GM015	Urinary infection	100	16.40	1640
GM016	Gastroenteritis	80	20.40	1632
GM017	Headache	100	12.47	1247
GM018	Peptic ulcer	80	14.40	1152
GM019	Syncope	80	9.37	750
GM020	Viral illness	100	3.60	360
	Other inpatient	870		25 398
GM099	General medicine standard bed day	39 962	1.36	54 348
				181 340

| Prepared by | Noel Austin | Version no | 0.2 |
| Authorized by | P M Blackmore/Kathryn O'Donnell | Date | 18-May-97 |

Figure 6.6: Service requirement: resource requirement worksheet: nursing.

Box 6.3: Service Level Agreement: typical contents

Unambiguous definition of service:	chest x-ray for immobile patient
How delivered:	mobile x-ray machine
Where delivered:	on ward
By whom:	radiology directorate
To whom:	general medicine directorate
When available:	8.00 a.m. to 10.00 p.m., 7 days a week
Response times:	4 working hours from request (e.g. a request made at 9.00 p.m. will be satisfied by 11.00 a.m. the next morning
How invoked:	telephone call from Senior Registrar or Consultant
Reporting:	written report by 10 a.m. following day
Quality measures:	90% of requests will be answered within 4 hours

---

As a result of this process of service delivery planning and resource aggregation you will now have a comprehensive estimate of the resources you need to deliver your key services. You can now adjust this estimate by an amount to reflect the services not covered by your service delivery planning process; a good rule of thumb is that if your key services consume 80 per cent of your bed-days they probably consume a similar proportion of your other resources too, so a simple arithmetic adjustment of 25 per cent to your calculated resource needs should give you a reasonable estimate of the total resources you need to run your directorate. You will need to make some provision for secretarial and other resources not covered by your service delivery plans, but you now have the basis

---

Box 6.4: Typical operational plan contents

Clients
Services provided
Contractual basis
Resources
Policy statements
Budgets
Management arrangements

for a resource-based budget and an operational plan (Box 6.4), which is really a summary of the service delivery plans, contracts, service level agreement, and policy statements which will guide the day-to-day operation of the directorate over the forthcoming time period together with the budget you will need to provide the service. We discuss the topic of budgeting in Chapter 7.

Risk management

David Bowden

Since it was formalized in the NHS six years ago, risk management has become an essential instrument for ensuring the operational success of NHS Trusts, health authorities, and general practices. It is a key diagnostic tool for assessing the state of health of the organization concerned, and it also provides a specific means of treating the risk situations identified.

The need for risk management

As the demands made on services continue to grow, so too do the pressures to create a more focused system for managing risk, in order to maintain and improve the quality of patient care, to enhance the safety of the services supporting that activity, and to reduce wasteful expenditure.

Not least amongst the reasons for needing to reduce risk is the growing level of clinical negligence litigation and the continuing imperatives of health and safety, environmental, and other legislation. By its very nature, health care is a risk activity. Indeed, doctors and other health professionals should not be discouraged from taking some risks in developing more effective methods of treatment and care for patients. But, it is important that such risks are taken as a result of a positive decision to do so, on the basis of good information and a sound understanding of the possible consequences and the likely outcome of treatment. Of course, whenever possible, this should be done with the knowledge and consent of the patient or patients concerned. Similarly, the most effective managers are those who are prepared to take calculated risks, deliberately choosing to make such judgements from a range of fully detailed options.

What is of concern is the wide range of risks which occur by accident rather than design and through mischance, mishap, or mistake. Even more worrying are those untoward incidents which result from the lack of clear policies, deficient working practices; poorly defined responsibilities; inadequate communications, and staff working beyond their competence. After all, most clinical negligence is not caused by individual clinical error, but as a result of that type of systems failure or a combination of several small mistakes occurring at the same time. The challenge for managers and clinicians alike is to eliminate, or at least reduce, the potential for such misfortunes by being proactive in the future management of risk. Why proactive? Because being reactive is simply not good enough. Whether considering a brain-damaged baby, the administration of the wrong drug, the absence of firefighting equipment, the lack of training in lifting techniques, or inadequacy of emergency generators, it is morally indefensible to say 'It was just one of those things', if it was possible to foresee and prevent the incident from happening – even once.

The cost of clinical risk

Quite apart from the quality-of-care issues involved, the potential cost of risk is very high. So far as NHS clinical negligence is concerned, the NHS now pays out over £150m every year. In 1994, the Merrett Group actuaries established a liability triangulation which highlighted dramatically how this will increase, year on year, unless action is taken. The claims triangulation was calculated with a seven-year tail, as many claims take this unacceptably long time to be settled.

The research indicated that a typical 1000-bed acute general hospital Trust in the NHS, with a bed occupancy rate of 89 per cent, can expect 5800 patient incidents per annum. A patient incident can range from the avoidable death of a patient, to someone simply falling out of bed or being given the wrong drug inconsequentially. Of this total, on average, only 116 will be potentially compensational events, of which 38 will become claims.

The cost of settling 50 per cent of those claims can be up to £2.6m (1993–94 costs), excluding legal and claims handling expenses. These costs are already too high for any Trust to maintain its financial viability. What is more worrying is the way in which the figures will evolve if the Trust does not take preventative action. It should be borne in mind that, in the past, many negligence claims have taken several years to settle, so that, based on the 1993–94 exposure of £2.6m:

- total payments will actually be £3.77m by 2000–01 (based on 10 per cent per annum inflation)

- the base figure for 2000–01 will become £5.76m without any change in the nature of the risks, but as a result simply of the increased frequency and cost of claims

- that base figure of £5.76m will give rise to total payments for the 2000–01 year of exposure of £16.29m (by 2007–08)

- payment made in the year 2007–08 will be £7.18m, and the outstanding liability will be £48.37m.

The elements of risk management

Risks are present within all health care organizations and inherently their services carry many vulnerabilities. It is therefore pleasing to note that the need to have a positive approach to risk management has now been fully recognized. In this respect, it is helpful to distinguish between the different elements which should form part of any risk management programme. The three aspects are shown in Box 6.5.

The nature of risk management

Positive attitudes

Risk management should always be regarded as a positive concept. Under no circumstances should it be equated with defensive medicine, which is costly, ineffective, and demeaning of noble professions. It is not about interfering with clinical freedom, although it can and should be used to pinpoint deficiencies which may need to be rectified. It should be seen as an extension to medical and clinical audit, and as part of the organization's approach to continuous quality improvement.

As the medical profession in the UK moves inexorably from a tradition of clinical freedom to evidence-based practice, systems have to be developed to determine the most effective processes of care. Allied to this is the need for safer systems which support the direct care activities. Audit and risk management provide a great opportunity to highlight and evaluate system failures and inefficiencies, and point the way to improved outcomes from the treatment and care processes.

Openness and honesty

For the services provided by a clinical directorate to become safer and more effective, the management of risk must become everyone's business. There must be an in-built discipline within the directorate and indeed with the Trust as a whole, which ensures that inevitably and without fail, any untoward incident, of whatever nature, is reported immediately. This can only happen if there are changes in the organization's value systems, leading to greater honesty and openness within the Trust, and a genuine willingness by all to admit to mistakes and to report their 'near misses'. This will enable untoward incidents to be managed and dealt with expeditiously and allow managers and clinicians to be proactive in giving patients and their relatives speedy, willing, and comprehensive explanations of any adverse outcomes of care. Not only will this lead to a minimization of patient distress, it will result in fewer complaints and claims for negligence, not more.

Key clinical risk concerns

Despite a growing acknowledgement among clinicians and managers of the importance of managing and controlling clinical risk, a hard core of fundamental

Box 6.5: The elements of risk management

1 Risk assessment
A clinical director cannot begin to manage the risks effectively, until he or she knows what the risks are.

Risk assessment is the process for identifying the actual and potential risk situations which exist within all or part of the organization, and analysing their impact in various ways. The outcome should be the creation of a risk profile and action plan, highlighting the top 10–20 issues for the most urgent attention.

This can often be achieved more quickly and objectively through an independent and unbiased risk audit survey.

2 Risk reduction and control
Staff in all clinical directorates manage risk every day. However, this is so often achieved on an *ad hoc* basis and in a very uncoordinated way. Risk management provides a framework in which risks are identified and dealt with more quickly and in a more focused way.

This can only be achieved if the clinical directors and other line managers within a Trust accept the management of risk as one of their key operational responsibilities.

The employment of a centrally-based risk manager will be enormously beneficial in initiating, coordinating, and driving the risk management agenda across the Trust. However, essentially he or she is there to support and advise the line managers on a day-to-day basis, and to monitor their successes in this respect.

3 Risk transference
The most likely method of cost transference is through insurance. NHS Trusts have always been free to obtain insurance cover for most risks. This is expected to be a combination of self-insurance and commercial insurance. The permitted insurance arrangements can cover property, motor, employer's liability, public and products liability, and directors' and officer liability.

Since 1 April 1995, NHS Trusts in England have also been encouraged to join the Clinical Negligence Scheme for Trusts (CNST), run by the NHS Litigation Authority. This allows the member Trusts to pool their contributions in order to be covered for any seriously expensive claim which is settled on their behalf.

Insurance cover does, of course, have many benefits, but it is only one element of the risk management process and is no panacea. What is of concern is its tremendous potential to encourage complacency, and the fact that, of itself, it does little positively to improve patient care.

It is therefore extremely encouraging that the CNST has developed 10–11 essential risk management standards which, if met, provide the incentive of reduced annual premiums to the scheme (see **Box 6.6**).

clinical risks continues to dominate the risk exposure of Trusts. The following issues represent the major risk issues observed by Merrett Health Risk Management risk managers as they regularly assess clinical risks.

A great deal of clinical risks occur because of *poor communications* between doctors and nurses/midwives in the same clinical team; senior staff and their juniors; professionals in one department and those in another; and between clinicians and their patients. The maxim is 'you haven't told them unless they've heard it'. Risks occur because of misguided communication, wrong information being given, indecipherable or inaudible information, or simply because there has been no communication.

The *reduction in junior doctors' hours* can create problems around handover and cover, where doctors from one speciality routinely cover for doctors in another. In such circumstances there can be a lack of specialized knowledge at a critical stage of a patient's care. Particular problems occur where there is *inadequate induction of locums or agency staff*.

Lack of *consent to treatment* continues to be a significant aspect in many actions for negligence. There is an urgent need for adequate information for patients on the risks of treatment and non-treatment and for the implementation of methods to ensure that patients have read and understood it, and have given their *informed consent*.

It can be said that, in general, *inexperience is no defence to an allegation of negligence*, and that, in essence, the standard of skill expected of a doctor would be that expected of practitioners with whom he or she claims to have similar skills. However, if an inexperienced doctor does not seek the advice of a senior or specialist when a prudent junior would do so, he or she may be considered negligent. Similarly, if novices undertake procedures in which they are not experienced, other than in an emergency, they are effectively claiming the skills of a suitably trained practitioner and will be judged on that standard.

The need for *adequate medical supervision* is still not being met satisfactorily in many hospitals, particularly at nights and weekends. Experience indicates that it is often at these times that incidents are likely to develop into real risk situations.

One of the fundamental pillars of any risk management process must be to ensure that standards of record keeping, record storage, and retrieval systems are high. It is disturbing to note that the majority of hospitals are still not reaching *adequate standards for medical records, particularly in respect of the compilation and content of records*.

The *inadequate interfacing between health care and social care* creates many risk situations, particularly in *mental health services and child protection services*. Such risks need to be addressed in an explicit way by both purchasers and providers of the care, in close dialogue with social service colleagues.

Many clinical risks occur as a result of a junior member of the clinical team being *unsure of* his or her *levels of responsibility and authority*, particularly in an emergency situation. A classic example concerns a senior house officer in the obstetric team not being absolutely certain what action he or she is able to take with a difficult birth, at a weekend, with the consultant 'on call' but miles away from the hospital. These circumstances need to be predicted in advance and talked through with all members of the team. Staff need to be clear exactly what is expected of them in a range of potentially difficult situations.

As obstetrics is the speciality which presents the greatest financial risks, there is a whole range of issues where clinicians and managers can improve processes and minimize risks. *Territorial disputes between obstetricians and midwives* can be due to lack of consultant input in a labour ward and delegation of duties to junior medical staff who are perceived by senior midwives to be less experienced than themselves. Inadequate timeliness of actions can lead to disastrous situations.

The *lack of adequate theatre policies and procedures* remains a constant backdrop to surgical services. While the majority of procedural failures may not in themselves cause major incidents, the *failure to report* them and correct them allows sloppy habits to continue. Where several procedural 'glitches' occur together and there is no failsafe mechanism, serious consequences may follow.

Finally, patients are able to sue NHS Trusts for failure to provide correct diagnosis/treatment. It is possible that a claim could succeed if a *delay in treatment* caused additional pain and suffering, death, or bodily injury to a patient, including a delay in treatment caused by an administrative problem. Clinical negligence can involve action or *inaction*, through advice given or *failure to advise*, and, therefore, through commission or *omission*.

The need to address the quality versus quantity versus cost equation

Many risks occur in the NHS setting because clinicians and others are having to make urgent decisions under pressure, or at least in the genuine belief that they are under pressure. Often, the nature of the decision is guided by intuition rather than an analysis of all the facts. Indeed, a detailed assessment is often not possible in an emergency situation. These daily decisions can be affected by an over-stretched operating theatre, an overcrowded A&E department, and an understaffed ward. In such circumstances, individual professionals are forced to make immediate, individual judgements about which patient to treat first, which patient to admit first, and which patients to discharge early. Such situations increase the risks to the patients concerned, to well in excess of the inherent risk involved.

To reduce the potential for increased risk in these situations, the Trust board concerned needs positively to address the whole quality versus quantity versus cost issue, involving a wide range of clinical views. It is necessary to ask the question 'Are there any circumstances in which the Trust would knowingly compromise the quality of patient care?' If the answer to the question is 'No', but the reality is that the quality of care is not up to the Trust's defined standards, then the Trust must decide whether or not to reduce the quantity of activity or to increase the funds available. However, if the answer is 'Yes', then the Trust board should recognize quite explicitly the quality deficiencies it accepts. Having reached its conclusion, the Trust will no doubt wish to debate the issue with its main purchasers of service.

This is not a simple or straightforward matter. Health care is, of course, a complex service industry. It is concerned with the quality of life, and with life and death issues. The debate needs to recognize the emotional and emotive aspects involved, and the delicate interdependence of the wide and multifaceted range of departments and functions. Nevertheless, unless these crucial issues are addressed, fundamentally, a vast range of risk situations will continue to occur on an *ad hoc* basis, and without any sense of control. This is no longer acceptable. Clinicians must be given clear guidance and support in this highly sensitive arena.

The spectrum of managing risk

The requirement is to have systems in place which will:

PREVENT risks occurring, or at least
ELIMINATE them if they have occurred, or
REDUCE their impact, and
CONTAIN the effects, or
CONTROL the risk factors, and
MINIMIZE the effects, and above all
MANAGE the risks.

It is, of course, also vital to learn the lessons from the errors which have occurred and to put in place practical means of avoiding the same circumstances in future.

Establishing a risk management process

The following are some key ingredients of a successful risk management process:

- secure top level commitment
- make it a line management responsibility (particularly clinical directors)
- take a more focused approach

- see it as a process not a programme
- be more explicit re what to expect of staff
- achieve attitudinal and behavioural change re honesty and openness
- staff need to feel valued
- invest in training and education
- establish performance review
- address quality vs quantity vs cost equation
- be proactive and positive.

The development of a meaningful risk management strategy endorsed by the Trust or the health authority board, is a crucial first step in setting the above framework (Box 6.6). In the undertaking of a detailed risk assessment and the creation of a prioritized risk profile of the services concerned, audit is also vital in identifying the most important and urgent existing risk issues to tackle.

Conclusion

The consequences of not taking the management of risk seriously are that Trusts and clinical directorates will continue to have quality deficiencies, and to pay claims, fines, additional staff costs, additional replacement costs, and extended stay costs. There will also be unexpected litigation and unplanned losses of facilities and services, resulting in the need for managers to realign their priorities constantly – a difficult enough task at the best of times. On the other hand, the benefits of a risk management programme are:

- improvements in the quality of patient care
- reduction in damage and injury to patients
- enhanced security and safety of buildings and equipment
- better environment for staff
- reduction in wasteful expenditure
- increases in patient activity.

All of us do, and should, take risks. The imperative is that managers and clinicians together must identify, analyse, and control the risk appropriately, and to take decisions on risk reduction through informed choice and judgement. By being positive and proactive in the management of this future uncertainty, they can play a crucial part in securing a continuous improvement in the quality of patient care.

Box 6.6: The Clinical Negligence Scheme for Trusts: the risk management standards

1 The Board has a written risk management strategy that makes their commitment to managing clinical risks explicit.

2 An Executive Director of the Board is charged with responsibility for clinical risk management, throughout the Trust.

3 The responsibility for management and coordination of clinical risk is clear.

4 A clinical incident reporting system is operated in all medical specialties and clinical support departments.

5 There is a policy for rapid follow-up of major clinical incidents.

6 An agreed system of managing complaints is in place.

7 Appropriate information is provided to patients on risks and benefits of the proposed treatment or investigation, and the alternatives available, before a signature on a consent form is sought.

8 A comprehensive system for the completion, use, storage, and retrieval of medical records is in place. Record keeping standards are monitored throughout the clinical audit process.

9 There is an induction/orientation programme for all new clinical staff.

10 A clinical risk management system is in place.

11 There is a clear documented system for management and communication throughout the key stages of maternity care.

7

Managing financially

Christopher J Cowton

> We didn't actually overspend our budget. The Health Commission allocation simply fell short of our expenditure.
>
> Keith Davis, Chairman, Wollongong Hospital, Australia, 1981

Money: resource or measure?

Money has always been important in health care. Staff need to be paid, buildings constructed and maintained, supplies purchased, and so on. Accounting systems have been needed to help ensure that the right sums of money are available and spent in accordance with proper authority. Quite reasonably, health care organizations have been required to act as good stewards of the large sums of money entrusted to them, and to account for that stewardship.

But money is not just a resource. Increasingly, it is the measure of many if not all things. This has been a central feature of recent changes in the overall system of health care in the UK, with increased financial independence and vulnerability at the organizational level and consequent changes in the management and financial visibility of individual organizational sub-units and activities. Thus a relatively simple concern with the management *of* finance in NHS organizations has been superseded, or at least supplemented, by what might be termed management *through* finance. More than ever, health care professionals find themselves bumping up against money issues and financial questions, and for this reason it is necessary for them to acquire a basic understanding of what accounting is about – if only to avoid being fooled by accountants! It is the aim of this chapter to help in this.

The scope of this chapter

A common perception of accounting is that it is not only boring (which of course isn't true!) but also 'difficult' – replete with abstruse terminology and complicated calculations. Certainly there are technical areas of accountancy that are complex and challenging, and it is not surprising that accountants have to undergo, as health care professionals do, a considerable period of training before they can be considered competent to practise in a professional capacity. Yet many of the basic principles and most important issues can be grasped without delving too deeply into the detail. This chapter falls into two main sections:

1 *Understanding financial statements*, which (a) examines the principles behind the new types of financial statements now being produced in the NHS, and (b) indicates how those statements might be analysed to provide useful insights

2 *Managing costs and budgets*, which explains how accountants think about costs and how those ideas can be used when managing financially.

The focus will be upon understanding general principles rather than present, and possibly ephemeral, practice. Terms considered to be significant in the context of accounting are italicized when they are first used. Constraints on space mean that a considerable amount of detail will have to be sacrificed, but guidance on obtaining further up-to-date and detailed information is provided at the end of the chapter.

Understanding financial statements

The NHS has been moving away from traditional public sector accounting, based on receipts and payments of cash, to an approach similar to that in the private sector, which employs the *accruals* concept for its major financial statements – though cash flow statements are still important. Briefly, the accruals concept means that the financial impact of transactions and some other events is recognized as they occur, which is not necessarily the same time as the associated cash flow takes place – the cash flow could be earlier or later. Thus we have moved away from a focus on *receipts and payments* to *income and expenditure*. These may sound like similar terms but they actually mean very different things. For example, in accruals accounting supplies are counted as a cost when they are used, not when they are paid for. The easiest way to see what the new approach consists of, why it might be intuitively appealing, and the issues it raises, is to work through a simple example.

Stocks, cash, and profit

Entreprenurse: day one

> Suppose that a nurse finds herself in financial difficulties and decides to go into business selling cans of drink by the roadside in her spare time. In order to start up her business, 'Entreprenurse', she uses £10 that she has available to purchase 50 cans

of drink at 20p each. During the day she sells 30 cans for 30p each, making a revenue of £9. Has she done badly or well? In cash terms she is down £1 on the day. This is perfectly *accurate*, but because she also has 20 more cans – her closing stock – than she did at the start of the day, it also seems to be an *incomplete* indicator of her performance. There is more to assessing the performance of the business than simply looking at the cash dimension. How well she has done depends on whether, and if so by how much, the deterioration in her cash position is outweighed by the improvement in her 'can position'. If we can put a value on the cans we will be able to come up with an overall measure of her performance.

The use of money as a common denominator is a particularly strong integrating feature of accounting, facilitating the management of disparate activities, and is one of the reasons for its important role in the management of contemporary organizations. Accountants generally value stock at cost, which in this case is easy enough to ascertain. Thus a simple depiction of her performance could be calculated as follows, with the brackets indicating a negative figure:

Entreprenurse: stocks, cash, and profit

	£
Change in cash	(1.00)
Change in stock (20 cans @ 20p)	4.00
Surplus	3.00

Annual income twenty pounds, annual expenditure nineteen nineteen six, result happiness. Annual income twenty pounds, annual expenditure twenty pounds ought and six, result misery.

Mr Micawber in David Copperfield by Charles Dickens

Given that the nurse presumably expects to sell the stock the next day, valuing it merely at cost may look a little harsh, but imagine what would happen if it were valued at its expected resale value – the net result (or profit) would be improved simply by buying more stock, not by actually selling it. Accountants are not impressed by this and will recognize the profit only when the critical event in its generation has taken place. They will occasionally value stock at its net realizable value (i.e. selling price less the expenses involved in the anticipated sale), but only if it happens to be lower than cost. The 'lower of cost and net realizable value' rule in valuing stock is an example of the application of *prudence*, a basic concept that accountants carry around with them, which in this situation might be summed up as 'don't count your chickens before they've hatched'.

The above intuitive calculation of a surplus of £3 is, in effect, the difference between two 'snapshots' of the business; the first just after she had invested some money in the business but before she had bought the cans, the other at the end of the day. Accountants produce a particular type of snapshot called the *balance sheet* – which technically is a summary of the various balances contained in the books of account at a particular point in time. A balance sheet for Entreprenurse at the end of day one is shown below.

Entreprenurse: balance sheet as at end of day one

	£
Stock	4.00
Cash	9.00
	13.00
Capital	10.00
Retained profits	3.00
	13.00

It sounds extraordinary, but it's a fact that balance sheets can make fascinating reading.

Mary Archer, quoted in the *Independent*, 7 January 1989

This balance sheet is in *vertical* format, although we still tend to refer to the *sides* of the balance sheet. Stock and cash are both on the asset side. Note that 'capital' is not. In a sense the business, Entreprenurse, is in the nurse's debt, having received benefit (the initial investment of £10) from her. It is as if she has two pockets, one for herself and one for the business. Similarly, the retained profits are not on the asset side of the balance sheet, for the nurse has left the surplus in the business thus enhancing its financial capital.

Rather than the intuitive method used earlier, a more conventional way in which to calculate the profit would be to draw up a *profit and loss account*. Unlike a balance sheet, which is a snapshot at a point in time, the *P&L* account is a summary statement for a period.

Entreprenurse: profit and loss account for day one

	£
Turnover	9.00
Cost of sales	(6.00)
Profit	3.00

Thinking that he might be dealing with a simpleton, the chief executive asked his finance director, 'What does two plus two equal?' Quick as a flash came back the astute, if not ethical, reply, 'What do you want it to equal?'

The turnover, or total sales revenue, requires no explanation. However, it should be noted that the cost of sales figure is not the amount spent on purchases but rather the cost of the cans actually represented in the turnover figure; in other words, 30 cans at 20p each. This is an example of the *matching* principle, another fundamental component of accruals accounting. An attempt is made to match with a given set of revenues the costs associated with generating those revenues.

The relationship with purchases is often seen in the following form. The figures for day one of Entreprenurse have been inserted.

Entreprenurse: cost of sales for day one

		£
Opening stock		0.00
Purchases		10.00
		10.00
Less Closing stock		(4.00)
Cost of sales		6.00

Accountants are the witch doctors of the modern world.

Mr Justice Harman, Miles v. Clarke, 1953

The opening stock plus additions purchased during the period represent the total cost of cans available for sale during the period. The difference between that figure and any left over (closing stock) equals the amount sold. Alternatively, if the amount used is known the amount of current/closing stock (or at least what it should be) can be calculated. Incidentally, this pattern is a very familiar one in accounting, being used in all sorts of contexts.

A similar pattern occurs in the assigning of costs to a particular period. Many large payments are made for periods that do not coincide with an organization's accounting period. For example, a rental payment might be made for six months in advance on 1 November, yet the financial year end might be 31 December. In this case only one-third of the payment relates to the current year and would be included in the P&L account. The other, *unexpired* two-thirds would appear on the balance sheet as a *prepayment*, usually with debtors, to be charged subsequently to next year's P&L account. A prepayment is a form of asset, in the sense that it is a benefit to be carried forward to be used next year, just as closing stock or closing cash are.

Having dealt with the accounting issues that arise from the Entreprenurse's first day of business, it is time to examine events on day two, but first note again that the balance sheet is a 'snapshot' – it relates to a particular point in time – whereas the profit and loss or income and expenditure account sums up activity for a particular period. Indeed, the profit and loss account can be thought of as providing the link between two successive balance sheets. Note, too, that profit is not the same as cash surplus, so making profits does not necessarily mean that there is cash to spend.

Debtors and creditors

Entreprenurse: day two

With market awareness of Entreprenurse growing, sales on day two increase to 40 cans, although ten of these are to friends who promise to pay later in the month. Our nurse trusts her friends, and in any case it seems to her that it would be hypocritical to refuse for, of the 40 cans she has bought that day, 20 were on credit. The only problem is, how should these events be reflected in the financial statements of Entreprenurse drawn up at the end of day two?

First, we will deal with the issue of the sales on credit. Although the discussion of the accounts for day one might have left the impression that accruals accounting is more pessimistic or negative in its overtones than simple cash accounting, this is not always the case. Accountants are willing to recognize sales on credit as revenue (some eggs as chickens, even though unhatched!) for the period even if payment has not actually been received. Therefore it makes no difference to the P&L account whether Entreprenurse receives cash or promises. However, since the cash has not actually been received it cannot appear in the balance sheet. Instead, a figure for debtors is included. Like cash, this is an asset. Similarly, purchases on credit are treated like purchases for cash, except that a liability appears in the balance sheet, indicating that the business owes money. The financial statements for the second day's trading are shown below.

Entreprenurse: profit and loss account and balance sheet for day two

Profit and loss account for day two		Balance sheet as at end of day two	
	£		£
Turnover	12.00	Stock	4.00
Cost of sales	(8.00)	Debtors	3.00
		Cash	14.00
Profit	4.00		
		Current assets	21.00
		Creditors	(4.00)
		Net current assets	17.00
		Capital	10.00
		Retained profits	7.00
			17.00

The P&L account is no different from day one, except for reflecting the increased scale of operations. More can be said about the balance sheet, though, which has developed significantly. There are now three types of *current asset* – that is, cash or other assets that are expected to change form (principally into cash) during the coming year. It is conventional to list them in increasing order of liquidity. From these has been subtracted the figure for *creditors*, a form of *current liability*. The total of current assets less current liabilities is known as *net current assets* or *working capital*. The treatment of creditors as being, in effect, a negative asset, is very common today. Previously, the figure for creditors would have been added to the liabilities side of the balance sheet.

Finally, note that *retained profits* – sometimes slightly confusingly identified as 'profit and loss account', since it is the balance in that account – has grown to £7, which is the £4 profit from day two (none of which has been withdrawn from the business by the nurse) added to the balance *brought forward* of £3. This balance will be *carried forward* to the next balance sheet.

Fixed assets and depreciation

Entreprenurse: day three

Encouraged by the success of the first two days' business, our nurse decides to buy a small table for £1 from a local second-hand shop. The purchase of the table, which we will treat as a *fixed asset*, enables her to display her wares to better effect. This appears to pay off, for sales for the day amount to 60 cans. This results in a drop in closing stock, for she bought only 50 cans that morning.

The purchase of fixed assets (*capital items* such as equipment or buildings), with the intention of using them over a number of years, is referred to as *capital expenditure*. In the NHS, all other expenditure is referred to as *revenue expenditure*. The latter includes some items which, although they will be used for a number of years, are not considered to have a sufficiently high purchase price to warrant treatment as a fixed asset. They are simply *written off* to the income and expenditure account in the year of purchase and not *capitalized* for inclusion in the balance sheet.

Capital expenditure is a major area where cash accounting and accruals accounting diverge. Assuming that the asset is bought outright, cash accounting shows the full cost of the investment as a payment in the relevant financial period. However, accruals accounting spreads the cost of the asset over a number of periods. This is nothing to do with the manner in which the purchase of the asset is financed (remember, we are assuming that it has been paid for). Rather, it represents an attempt to match the cost of the asset to the periods in which it is going to be used. This matched element of total cost is called *depreciation*. In order to calculate the depreciation charge, four things need to be known:

1 the *cost* of the asset. This might seem easy, but there is often more to getting an asset working productively than simply buying it. Expenses such as design fees or commissioning costs might need to be capitalized as well

2 its likely *useful life*. This will often be shorter than its technological life. Many pieces of equipment are expected to be replaced by cheaper alternatives or a later generation of technology while they still work

3 its *scrap value*, if any, at the end of its useful life, less any costs involved in selling or decommissioning

4 the *depreciation method* which will be used to write off the net cost of the asset (1–3) over its assumed life (2). The most common method is the *straight line* method (Figure 7.1), which involves charging the same proportion of the net cost for each year of the asset's useful life. Also popular is the *reducing balance* method (Figure 7.2), which involves charging a constant proportion, not of the net cost,

but of the *net book value* (original cost less accumulated depreciation). It results in a relatively high depreciation charge in the early years, and much lower charges towards the end of the asset's useful life. One advantage of this method is that, at least for some assets, it tracks the way their second-hand value tends to decline, although there are considerable difficulties if the expected scrap value is zero or negligible – you can't find a depreciation rate that will get you to zero, and it has to be an extremely high rate if the expected scrap value is very low. You might also find, in the NHS, *usage-based* depreciation methods (Figure 7.3); the life of an asset, such as an x-ray tube, might be estimated in terms of hours of use, and depreciation charged according to the number of hours of usage in a particular period.

One of the intriguing features of depreciation is that, in accounting for the past, we have to make assumptions about the future. (It is not the only area of accounting

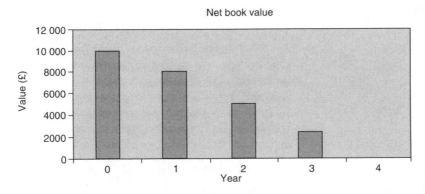

Figure 7.1: Straight line depreciation.

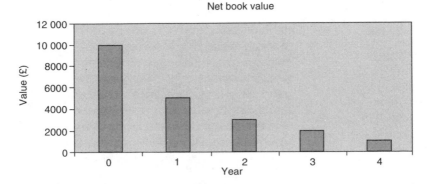

Figure 7.2: Reducing balance depreciation.

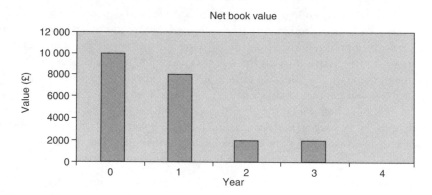

Figure 7.3: Usage-based depreciation.

where this is the case.) Like the shift from a cash basis to accruals accounting, this is another way in which accountants move beyond simple facts to report figures that, for some purposes at least, are considered to be more meaningful and useful.

Returning to the example of the table for Entreprenurse, the original cost of acquisition is £1. If we assume a zero scrap value and an expected useful life of ten days, we have a daily straight-line depreciation charge of 10p. (This asset is too cheap and too short-lived to be treated as fixed in practice; for the purposes of the current illustration it will have to do.) This is a cost in the P&L account for day three, shown below.

Entreprenurse: profit and loss account and balance sheet for day three

Profit and Loss Account for day three		Balance Sheet as at end of day three		
	£			£
Turnover	18.00	Table at cost		1.00
Cost of sales	(12.00)	*Less* Accum. deprecn.		(0.10)
		Net book value		0.90
Gross profit	6.00	Stock	2.00	
Depreciation	(0.10)	Debtors	3.00	
		Cash	21.00	
Net profit	5.90		26.00	
		Creditors	(4.00)	
		Net current assets		22.00
				22.90
		Capital		10.00
		Retained profits		12.90
				22.90

In the balance sheet, the depreciation that has been charged is subtracted from the original cost of the table to give its net book value. If we were to look at day four, another 10p would be charged in P&L account and the *accumulated depreciation* figure would grow to 20p, giving a written down value for the table of 80p.

Note that although the net figure against the asset in the balance sheet declines over its life, the net book value is not necessarily what the ageing asset is worth (e.g. its second-hand value or what it would cost you to replace it with an asset in similar condition). However, in the published accounts of large companies you will sometimes find assets such as land and buildings valued, not on a *historical cost* basis, as in the example, but on a *current value* basis (or similar). In the NHS it is standard practice to substitute for the original historical cost the replacement cost of assets and to base depreciation on that, using methods explained earlier. This gives rise to a number of technical accounting issues which need not concern us here – for example, the increase on the asset side of the balance sheet has to be matched by an increase on the liabilities side, in the form of a *revaluation reserve*, otherwise the balance sheet would not balance! What is more significant is that the written down value of assets has more chance of bearing some relation to their worth than if the historical cost convention had been adhered to, particularly if there has been significant inflation since the capital item was purchased.

What should be apparent from the above is that depreciation itself does not involve any real cash outflow. Without anything else happening (like someone paying you a sum of money equivalent to your depreciation) it is merely a bookkeeping exercise, not an economic transaction. Having charged depreciation does not, in itself, mean that when the asset has worn out you will have the money to replace it. So why do it if you're in a situation where no-one hands over money for doing it? Is it just an unnecessary complication brought about when cash accounting is superseded by accruals accounting? A number of possible reasons could be given, but one is apparent by considering our Entreprenurse example again. The cash flow on day three is going to look worse than on the following days simply because it was the day on which the table happened to be bought. Yet the table is going to be doing its work on those other days too (imagine if it had been rented instead of bought outright). It seems 'unfair' for day three to carry that burden. Any attempt to judge the trend of the business from a receipts and payments statement would have to be careful to take account of the capital expenditure in day three and make an appropriate mental adjustment. Depreciation within an accruals accounting framework helps to do that within the figures, charging the cost of the asset to the periods in which benefits are expected to flow from it. More generally, the capitalization and depreciation of assets, backed up by a proper assets register, provides a disciplined framework for knowing what assets are owned – which is not something that parts of the NHS have traditionally been strong at.

When a fixed asset is disposed of, the sale proceeds (which are a form of capital income) may not equal the written down amount shown in the books of account, in which case a surplus or loss, or adjustment to depreciation, will arise. Such figures are not necessarily of much significance of themselves, for they are simply a function of the choice of depreciation method and assumptions made. What is important is whether the disposal represented a good deal given the state of the asset and market conditions.

Finally, note that in drawing up the financial statements we have assumed that the future of Entreprenurse looks reasonably secure; that it is a *going concern*, to use accountants' terminology. But having brought out the main features of accruals accounting by focusing upon the first three days of business, we will ignore that supposed future and turn instead to the analysis of financial statements, sometimes referred to as *ratio analysis*.

Financial statement analysis

The most important requirement for interpreting financial statements is to understand what the basic figures mean. This has been the aim of the chapter so far. Only then is it time to try to wring out of them some more insights. Contrary to the implication of the exposition in many accounting textbooks, financial statement analysis is not a rule-bound area. While there are certain 'standard' things that can be done, even when analysing publicly listed companies the particular form that the analysis will take depends on the nature of the business and the perspective from which it is being conducted, e.g. shareholder, supplier, credit rating agency, etc. You can calculate whatever ratios you want, as long as you have some idea of what they might show you. Many of the ratios that might seem obvious to someone who works in a particular line of business do not appear in textbooks, which are attempting to generalize across different industry sectors. Different writers categorize ratios in different ways. Common categories include:

- *performance* – measures of effectiveness

- *efficiency* – how well various resources have been used

- *liquidity* – ability to meet short-term financial commitments

- *financial structure* – how the enterprise is financed, indicating its solvency.

Since a ratio is simply the arithmetic relationship between two numbers, and since those numbers can come from a number of sources, ratios can take a number of forms:

- two figures from the income and expenditure account, e.g. a profit margin (profit divided by revenue) or a cost ratio (a particular cost divided by total costs or revenue)

- two figures from the balance sheet, e.g. the current ratio (current assets divided by current liabilities, indicating whether short-term financial obligations can be met)

- one figure from the income and expenditure account and one from the balance sheet, e.g. return on capital (profit divided by capital or net assets) or asset turnover (revenue divided by fixed or total assets, showing how well the assets are being managed to generate income). Since the I&E figure is for a period, but the balance sheet figure is for a point in time, you may wish to take the average of the balance sheet figures for the beginning and the end of the year, but this may be getting a little more sophisticated than the robustness of the figures or strength of possible conclusions warrant

- one figure from one of the financial statements and one from elsewhere, e.g. revenue per employee, cost per case.

Such 'ratios' may be expressed in a number of different ways:

- as a pure ratio, e.g. a current ratio of 2:1

- as a percentage, e.g. a return on capital of 6 per cent

- as a financial sum, e.g. £35 000 per employee

- as a number of times, e.g. an asset turnover of ten times per annum

- number of days, e.g. an asset turnover of 36.5 days, which is simply a different way of expressing the previous ratio.

Calculating ratios is one thing; understanding what they mean is another. A ratio in isolation means little or nothing. Some sort of yardstick is needed to indicate its significance. Norms, such as expecting a return on capital of 6 per cent, might provide such a yardstick. The derivation of norms is often problematic in theory, but if you have them imposed upon you, theoretical niceties suddenly melt away. When delving deeper into the financial statements, though, explicit norms are unlikely to be available, since it is common when setting overall targets in a devolved system of management to claim (at least) that it does not matter how those targets are reached; that is the responsibility of the local management. There are two useful things that can be done to judge the significance of the ratios you have calculated. First, the *trends* over time can be examined. While it might be difficult to specify, in absolute terms, what the level of a particular ratio should be, whether it is broadly in line with the past, has jumped significantly, or is drifting upwards or downwards gradually, is useful to know. Many managers find it useful to develop a spreadsheet program into which they can enter new figures as they appear. The major constraint on trend analysis tends to be the availability of figures for previous years. Recent re-organization can make it very difficult to judge whether things are getting better. Second, *comparisons* can be made with similar units. The considerations that apply to comparative analysis are the same as those that relate to trend analysis: are suitable data available; and are figures broadly in line or not?

The process of analysing financial statements, using both standard and customized ratios, is as much about raising questions as providing answers. An unusual change in a ratio might indicate a number of things, which examination of other ratios might help to clarify. Sometimes, though, it will simply raise a number of issues which cannot be resolved merely by more analysis of the statements before you. Other information will need to be collected, people talked to, or a more up-to-date picture of the situation obtained. In some ways analysing financial statements can be likened to the work of a detective – at least the fictional versions with which we are most familiar. There are certain standard clues one looks for, certain things one checks at the scene of the crime, but then it is a question of following up the interesting leads and pursuing the perplexing questions.

Interpreting financial statements is thus more a creative process than a mechanical one. The financial data and analysis have to be related to how the entity to which they refer actually works. It is not something to be left to the accountants alone. Moreover, while there are certain standard tools available, before diving into calculating ratios read the statements themselves. Scan over the various items and, using some rough mental arithmetic, note any striking increases or relationships. Note that one of the reasons for using ratios is to control for scale; entities of different size can be compared on a common basis. But size is still important, so note at the very beginning whether there has been any significant change in the extent of operations. Rapid change in scale can also temporarily disrupt a period's activities and make interpretation of highly summarized statements tricky, so it is worth checking for this before embarking on any analysis.

Managing costs and budgets

Financial statements, suitably analysed and interpreted, can perform a valuable targeting or monitoring function, helping to direct attention to important areas where decisions might need to be taken. However, while accounts might help to suggest the need or opportunity for a decision, it is rarely obvious from them which course of action should be taken. There are a number of reasons for this, the most important of which are:

- the routine financial statements are general purpose documents, whereas a particular decision usually requires a tailor-made analysis to see what difference it will make if a particular course of action is undertaken

- in particular, the accounts are focused upon the reporting entity's past, whereas making a decision is all about identifying, and then choosing between, alternative possible futures.

The accounts are likely to provide some useful information for making a decision, but this will need to be extrapolated forward, which requires judgement as to the reasonableness of doing so. And other information will, in all likelihood, also be needed. For example, you might need to do some market research or find out how the proposed course of action might impact upon costs. In the following section we will examine the standard approach that accountants take to understanding the behaviour of costs, before going on to consider budgets, pricing and business cases.

Opportunity cost

It hardly needs saying that the provision of health care incurs costs. Contrary to what might often be implied, costs are 'good things', for they represent the devotion of resources to patient care. The challenge is not simply to cut costs – for example by closing wards or cancelling operations – but to manage costs properly to the benefit of patients.

Opportunity costing is an approach that recognizes that there are limits to the sums that an individual or an organization can spend so that, in order to do one thing you have to make a conscious decision not to make another. The value of the thing forgone is the opportunity cost. For instance, you may decide that in order to re-model your kitchen at home you will have to forgo your skiing holiday. The value to you of the skiing holiday is the opportunity cost of re-modelling the kitchen.

The concept of opportunity cost is one coined by economists and extensively used as part of a complex battery of tools by health economists. However, it is a useful tool for assessing whether you are making the best use of your available money. Its use is best illustrated by a simple exercise conceived by Professor David Cohen of the University of Glamorgan, which consists of three stages:[1]

1 Imagine you have been asked to make a 10 per cent saving on your directorate budget. Which services would you stop providing and what resources would you get rid of to achieve this reduction?

2 Now imagine your directorate budget has been increased by 10 per cent. What additional services would you provide, and what additional resources would you acquire to provide them?

3 Finally, look at the two lists of services. Are there any services which you would provide in the good times which are actually more useful or valuable than the services you would stop providing in the bad times? If so, make the change now.

Opportunity costing is a useful way of evaluating the merits of competing proposals and of deciding whether to replace equipment.

Cost behaviour

In order to manage costs, it is useful to know what influences them. One of the most obvious *drivers* of total costs, which has traditionally been the focus of accountants' attention, is the volume of output or, more appropriately expressed in a health care setting, the level of activity (e.g. number of patients treated, tests conducted, or meals prepared). Costs can then be divided up into two types:

- *variable costs*, the total of which varies in proportion to activity level. Examples, in different health care settings, include drugs dispensed or food ingredients used. In the absence of further information, these are usually assumed to be constant per unit of activity

- *fixed costs*, which are expected to be unaffected by changes in activity level. Once committed they are often very difficult to change, at least in the short term. The average fixed cost per unit of activity falls as the level of activity rises.

Fixed costs can usefully be divided into two types:

- *capacity*, which are necessary for the unit to operate over the period being considered, e.g. managers' salaries, depreciation, and capital charges

- *discretionary*, which are not related to the occurrence of activity for the coming period, e.g. conference attendance.

Accountants' use of the word 'fixed' in relation to costs thus tends to have a particular technical meaning. It does not mean that a cost will not change, even in the period being considered. After all, costs will often turn out to be higher or lower than expected. What it does mean is that the cost is not expected to change as a result of changes in the level of activity. It also does not mean that the particular costs will remain fixed whatever the level of activity; merely that within certain practical limits – the so-called *relevant range* – they are not expected to change. However, if desired it is possible to introduce the notion of *stepped fixed costs*, or simply *step costs* (sometimes referred to as *semi-fixed* or *semi-variable costs*), which reflect the way costs may jump if activity goes above a certain level. For example, above a certain point a hospital might have to open an additional ward, with all the staffing and other costs that such a decision would entail. Virtually all fixed costs are stepped at some point, but it is only worth recognizing a step if it happens to be relevant to the analysis you're undertaking. Why complicate things if it doesn't add anything useful?

Total costs will usually comprise both fixed and variable elements. Indeed, so will a number of individual cost categories, much as a domestic telephone bill is made up of a charge for line rental (fixed) and a charge for units used (variable). This is reflected in the simple diagram below, which shows a 'platform' of fixed costs, to which is added an amount of variable costs to form total costs. A line for revenue has also been added, based on the assumption of a constant price per unit of activity.

Figure 7.4 is not a diagram of how the financial situation changes over the period, but rather an indication of what might happen given different assumptions about the level of activity. The slopes of the two total lines indicate that, as one would hope, price is greater than variable cost for each unit of activity. This difference is referred to as *contribution*; i.e. each additional unit of activity contributes to the payment of fixed costs (or, after a certain point, the accumulation of profits) a sum of money equal to the difference between the price received and the cost associated with providing a single unit. The level of activity at which total revenue is expected to equal total costs (and total contribution equals fixed costs) is the *break even (be) point*, and diagrams of this sort are often referred to as *break-even charts*. However, while the break-even point might be important, it need not be our only focus of interest, so the term *cost–volume–profit (CVP) chart* is preferred. For readers with a mathematical bent, the explanation in Box 7.1 may be of interest.

Clearly such a view of cost and revenue behaviour is a simplification entailing many assumptions. But the chart can be made more sophisticated. Step costs can be added, for example, or a kink built in if the variable cost per unit is expected to change beyond a particular level of activity. The revenue line can also be tailored to reflect the kinds of contracts held. Such adaptations of the standard chart might help it to model a particular situation more accurately, but there is likely to remain a further problem – uncertainty. Because CVP analysis is

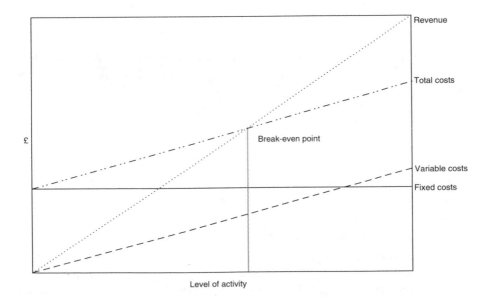

Figure 7.4: Cost–volume–profit chart.

Box 7.1: Calculating the break-even point

The chart has the algebraic form:
  $y = a + bx$
where
  y = total costs
  a = fixed costs
  b = level of activity
  x = variable cost per unit.

If p is price per unit and π stands for profit, then
  $\pi = px - bx - a$
    $= (p-b)x - a$
(p − b) is the contribution margin and (p − b)x the total contribution.

These simple relationships, plus adaptations, can be built into spreadsheet programs, or can be used directly to perform calculations. For example, since at the break-even point no profit or loss is made, it can be found by simply dividing fixed costs by the contribution margin, as proved below.

  $0 = (p - b)x^* - a$
  $\Rightarrow a = (p - b)x^*$
  $\Rightarrow x^* = a/(p - b)$

primarily a tool to help with planning, and the future is uncertain, there is a danger in drawing 'the' chart. In planning, it is better to address uncertainty than to assume it away. It is a good idea, then, to put the CVP analysis into a spreadsheet program. This facilitates sensitivity analysis, or the posing of 'what if?' questions, for example:

- what if the pay settlement turns out to be higher than we are expecting; will we still cover our fixed costs?

- what if the GP fundholding contract that we are hoping for doesn't come in at the right price, or we lose it altogether; where will that leave us?

- what is the *margin of safety*, that is, the amount by which anticipated activity may decrease before a loss results?

The robustness of particular decisions and positions with regard to key assumptions can quickly be checked, and further information obtained or action taken as a result. This is not a mere accounting exercise. It is a process in which all responsible professionals should take an interest and to which all available knowledge of how things work should be brought.

The use of a spreadsheet program also overcomes another limitation of the chart. To be able to draw the lines assumes either a single activity or, in a multi-activity setting, a constant mix over a range up to capacity. However, that is frequently not the case. Indeed, activity mix, whether cases, meals, or whatever, may be one of the major decisions to be made. Using a spreadsheet program enables a *financial model* to be built that accommodates the financial characteristics of each activity and permits the impact of alternative mixes to be studied.

Thus CVP analysis is, in essence, a simple tool that enables us to picture in financial terms the business unit that we are interested in and, armed with a better understanding of how it performs financially under various conditions, to manage it better. Clearly, one of the major areas to which this understanding can make a contribution is budgeting.

Budget preparation

One of the major features of a shift from the management *of* finance to management *through* finance, discussed in the introduction, is the delegation of budgetary responsibility. Like accounting in general, budgets are an increasingly important tool in a more diffuse system of management, rather than something of concern principally to the accountants. So if you are not already, get involved!

The most important thing in preparing the annual budget is to understand how costs are affected by what you do, which was the focus of the previous section. But there are other things that you will want to know. If it has not been forthcoming already, obtain some guidance from the centre about major planning assumptions that you should take into account, for example over the likely level of inflation in various costs or possible developments or contractions in the market. Don't think you have to be the expert about everything, just because it comes within your own area of budgetary responsibility. If there are 'significant others' who influence your activities, try to find out what they are thinking. And if you are willing to listen to them, involve your own people. They might know more than you do about a number of crucial issues. If done properly, this involvement should have the added benefit of increasing their interest in the budget, and their commitment to it.

One of the problems with budgeting is that it can become something of a ritual. This leads to two particular problems. First, budgets become characterized by *incrementalism*; that is, by far the biggest influence on next year's budget is this year's, and all the discussion and negotiation takes place over marginal changes. The core of the budget is neither challenged nor justified. One antidote to this is to look more fundamentally at what is in the budget, perhaps using a *zero-base budgeting* approach (ZBB). As its name implies, nothing is sacred with ZBB. Everything has to be justified from scratch. Unfortunately, perhaps, this is rarely possible; the budget might notionally have a zero-base, but the rest of the organization, with its traditions and power structures, is still there – although the contracting environment helps to focus the mind. Furthermore, an annual attempt at ZBB might be too disruptive, if taken to the limit. But its underlying message is still important. Perhaps one way to take it on board is to change the way in which budgets are reviewed. For example, instead of every clinical directorate's budget receiving the same degree of examination, an alternative approach is to subject one or two, on a random basis, to particularly painstaking analysis – 'pour encourager les autres'! If this seems inappropriate, at the very least it is important to link the budget to other business planning processes that take place. This might seem an obvious point, but it is surprising how often the budgeting process becomes decoupled from the other exercises by which organizations contemplate their future.

When preparing a budget, you have to decide where to start. The most appropriate point is either the amount of work you think you are likely to be asked to do next year, or your capacity if you think that it is less than the possible demand. Since budgeting is an iterative process, though, starting at the wrong point can usually be rectified later. Once you have some idea of workload – quantity, mix, and (possibly) pattern over time – you then have to work out the resources necessary to fulfil it and the likely cost of those resources. Useful inputs to this part of the process include:

- an understanding of cost behaviour

- knowledge of trends over recent years

- knowledge of what has been happening elsewhere

- possible inflationary factors

- recognition of the impact of recent decisions, such as the acquisition of new capital items (it is easy to fail to relate capital and revenue budgets to each other).

All this then needs to be related to pricing, which is one of the major reasons for budgeting in the era of the NHS internal market.

Pricing

Pricing is unusually important in NHS budgeting because, unlike much commercial pricing, it is strictly regulated. Cross-subsidization (to the extent that it can be identified) is banned and prices are restricted so that no more than a 6 per cent return on capital assets, valued on a current cost basis, is earned after charging depreciation. Prices are supposed to equal costs, which means that costing is used to set prices (it might not in commerce) and the majority of these prices are set annually. But what is the cost of a particular service? We can begin to answer this question by recalling the material on cost behaviour discussed earlier.

The most obvious costs in providing a service, such as a particular operation, are the variable costs. If we were to set our prices according to *marginal costing* these would be the only costs that we would take into account. If there were any other costs, as there certainly would be, we would make a loss and also contravene official regulations, which demand *full costing*. In the internal market, providers are required to recover all costs (including capital costs). Thus it is necessary when calculating prices to take fixed costs into account. Some of these will arise within the clinical directorate itself, but there are also significant *overhead* costs relating to the centre and support departments to be taken into account. These need, ultimately, to be *allocated* to, and hence recovered from, particular activities for which charges are levied.

It is not obvious how to allocate most overheads because, by definition, there is not a simple causal connection between their incurrence and the provision of a particular unit of service. What is usually sought is some sort of fair or equitable allocation, but since this is a matter of judgement, it is also open to negotiation – which can often become quite heated! However, there are some obvious ways of doing things, a few examples of which are given in Box 7.2.

Box 7.2: Examples of allocation bases

Overhead cost	Possible allocation basis
Heating and lighting	Floor space occupied by directorate
Finance department	Directorate total direct costs
Personnel department	Directorate salary bill
Portering	Number of beds

Although the suggestions in Box 7.2 might seem reasonable, they are susceptible to dispute. For example, a clinical director with a relatively low number of patient movements per bed per period might object to the basis for allocating portering costs. And remember, there is no immediate causal connection being implied here. Closing a particular clinical directorate would not be expected to lead to a saving in the amount of fixed overhead allocated to it, although there might be some marginal savings. We are simply seeking a basis that seems reasonably fair and satisfies external parties.

The second stage in the process is to attach those central overheads that have been allocated to the clinical directorate, together with any fixed costs of the directorate itself, to particular areas of activity or contracts. Some fixed costs arising within the directorate will be identifiable with, and hence *traceable* to, particular activities or contracts (especially if a marginal contract triggers a step cost), but most will simply need to be allocated. Note that one of the fixed costs to be included is depreciation (unless it is being treated as variable by means of a usage-based depreciation rate). Including an element for depreciation in the contract price amounts to charging for the use of assets in providing the service. But this does not mean that you will therefore be able to replace that asset when the asset has worn out. That will depend on the funds' actually being available and your being able to put together a sufficiently strong business case when the time comes.

In dealing with fixed overheads, you may also come across ideas associated with *activity-based costing*, which has in recent years received a great deal of attention and which is being promoted vigorously by management consultants. An exposition of the conveniently named *ABC* is beyond the scope of this chapter (although the technique may be less different from what has been described above than is sometimes claimed), but further information can be obtained from the contacts given at the end of the chapter.

Managing to budget

Some organizations seem to spend a considerable amount of time and effort on budgeting and other planning exercises and then, once they are completed, do little with them apart from file them. In the context of the NHS as it is today, that seems unwise. But in the absence of positive action on your part, there is a danger that your behaviour will approximate this. In the midst of a busy life, you will have to make an effort to find time to manage your finances. This will involve setting aside time to understand your financial monthly statements. If they arrive late, you can't understand them, or they do not provide the information you want (perhaps making a comparison with budget difficult), chase up your accountant. If you find yourself performing certain calculations regularly, ask if they can be provided as a matter of routine. And if you receive hard copy of figures and then have to have them put into a spreadsheet program, see if they can be provided in a form that would enable you to input them directly.

The difference between a budget figure and the actual outcome is called a *variance*. Variances may be *favourable*, if they are better than budget, or *unfavourable* or *adverse* if they are worse. Any variance that you judge to be significant – which might include some favourable ones – should be followed up. What you judge to be significant will depend on your view of the importance of a budget category and its inherent variability, but it might be worth setting down, in advance, certain margins of tolerance based on percentage of budgeted cost and/or absolute size. If you do decide to investigate a particular variance, try to get a breakdown of the figures underlying it. Variances can arise for a number of reasons, giving rise to different appropriate responses:

- the volume of activity might have turned out to be different from expected. Sometimes this is because the monthly budget is simply a twelfth of the annual budget, whereas the level of activity might be expected to show seasonal variation. Some more sophisticated systems take this into account by *profiling* the budget, in which case volume-related variances will be reduced. And some reporting systems factor out volume changes anyway, whether caused by seasonal variation or not, by *flexing* the original budget to reflect the actual, rather than budgeted, level of activity. In other words if, in setting the budget, you had known what you know now about the level of activity, what would the budget have looked like, *ceteris paribus*? Flexing saves having to remove the volume element from a variance so that you can concentrate on any other influences that may have been at work, but it should not be allowed to blind you to the importance of volume as an important factor to manage

- the overall level of activity might have proved to have been broadly in line with predictions, but the mix of activities might have turned out differently

- the amount and/or mix of resources used in delivering a particular workload might have been different from expected

- the price of resources might have differed from original budget estimates.

Sometimes you will be able to take corrective action, but often the result of your investigations will show that there is nothing to be done because the source of the variance is outside your control. Particularly where it looks like a significant adverse variance is going to result at the end of the financial year, it is worth letting the appropriate people know as soon as possible. Bad news is seldom welcome, but most managers hate late surprises. Countervailing measures may need to be taken and forecasts revised. Finally, always try to see a variance from budget not just as something which needs to be dealt with in order to keep this year's finances under control, but also as an opportunity to reflect and consider whether there might be lessons for how you set next year's budget, when it all begins again.

Capital investment

Perhaps the one financial management arena in which senior doctors have been active for a long time is that of capital investment. The traditional means of deciding on investment in medical equipment has been the Medical Equipment Committee, which has made its decisions on the basis of medical priorities and horse-trading, and not often on the basis of the value to the hospital as a whole of the proposed investment. The strictures of the new financial management regime have consigned this approach to history, and such decisions are now based on a sound financial evaluation of the alternatives together with the constraint imposed by the NHSE that all new investments must generate a return at a rate currently set at 6 per cent per annum.

Despite the new freedom to raise loans accorded to Trusts, in any Trust there will probably always be a greater demand for investment monies than the Trust can supply. The implication of this is that directorates will be competing with each other, or perhaps even internally, for a share of a limited sum. The Trust board will always adjudicate between investment proposals on the basis that they will approve the proposals which are in the best interests of the Trust as a whole; if clinical directors can agree which proposals should be adopted the resulting board decision is likely to be clinically and financially better informed than if they are unable to do so.

A relatively recent departure in Government funding of the NHS and other branches of the public sector has been the Private Finance Initiative (PFI). This envisages that NHS Trusts will seek to collaborate with private sector organizations in the funding and development of both clinical and support services (Box 7.3). The attraction for the private sector is seen to be the opportunity to invest in those parts of the service which are capable of generating profitable income and, for the Trust, the involvement of skilled commercial operators in the development of facilities which will strengthen the Trust's financial position and result in an improvement of the quality of service delivered to patients, staff, and other customers.

Box 7.3: Examples of collaboration with the private sector

New hospital
Car parks
Residences
Shopping precincts
Service development

Business cases

Most clinical directors will already have been through the often painful process of developing a business case to support an application for capital investment in service development. Most Trusts have developed formal structures and procedures for business cases, and this is an inevitable consequence of the need to be able to adjudicate between proposals on the basis of best fit to the Trust's overall needs by comparing them according to a common set of criteria.

The contents of a typical business case, as shown in Box 7.4, reflect the fact that the one-off cost of a capital investment is only a part of the total costs to which the Trust will be committed; as illustrated by the unopened wards and under-utilized equipment commonplace in the NHS until quite recently. Box 7.4 also illustrates that, in order to evaluate a capital investment proposal, it is necessary to have a clear understanding of the potential of the investment to generate income.

You may well have to do some market research in order to establish the demand for the proposed service and the price customers are prepared to pay for it. It is also important to assess the on-going costs of the proposed service, including staff, training, consumables, and maintenance. And even if you have shown that the proposed investment makes sound financial sense, there is no guarantee that you will be given the go-ahead, because another directorate's proposals may present an even stronger case.

Box 7.4: Contents of a typical business case

Capital investment
Revenue implications
Staff costs
Maintenance costs
Consumables
Cost of resultant service
Purchaser demand
Purchaser's price expectations

Replacements

Perhaps the largest proportion of investment monies goes to replace worn out, damaged, or obsolescent equipment. It is natural to assume that if you have been using a piece of equipment regularly for a long time, when it ceases to operate you should replace it. But is this really the case? There is a simple set of questions you should ask before committing yourself to the expenditure:

- do we still want to carry out the function performed by this equipment?
- is there a better way of doing it?
- have we chosen the best equipment for the job?
- can we fund it by saving elsewhere?
- is this the best way of spending the available money?

Conclusion: the end of the beginning

Within the constraints of a short chapter it has been possible to indicate only the most important features of a limited number of financial and accounting perspectives and tools. It was not intended to cover *all you ever needed to know about finance* – although it is possible that it has covered somewhat more than you ever *wanted* to know about it! However, having grasped the essentials of the subject, if you do wish to read further you would be well advised to look at the title mentioned under the heading of 'Further reading'.

Finally, the people who should know the most about how finance and accounting function where you work are the finance professionals themselves. Try to engage in dialogue with them. This might not always seem easy, but you should now feel more confident about asking them questions and will have more chance of understanding their replies. If you don't at least try to talk to them, you probably get the information – and the accountants – you deserve!

Reference

1 Cohen D. (1994) Marginal analysis in practice: an alternative to needs assessment for contracting health care. *BMJ*. **309**: 781–5.

Further reading

Mellett H, Marriott N and Harries S. (1993) *Financial management in the NHS: a manager's handbook*. Chapman & Hall.

While there are many other accounting books on the market, this has the obvious merit of being focused on the NHS. Both the examples it gives and the technical accounting factors that it reflects make it a valuable aid for any health care professional who wishes to acquire a sound grasp of accounting and finance.

Several specialist guides, which are often a good source of up-to-date technical material, are also published by some of the professional accounting bodies. It is worth contacting them for a list of currently available titles:

- Chartered Institute of Management Accountants, 63 Portland Place, London W1N 4AB, tel. 0171 637 2311;
- Chartered Institute of Public Finance and Accountancy, 3 Robert Street, London WC2 6BH, tel. 0171 543 5600.

8

Information

Noel Austin

At the start of this chapter it is important to stress that, when we talk about information, we are not talking just about information on computer systems. During your daily working life you probably make use of a wide variety of sources of information, such as patients' notes, lab reports, medical journals, and Trust computer systems; when you make decisions, they are quite commonly based on a combination of one or more of these. It is not the purpose of this chapter to discuss clinical information, although when we come to talk about resource management information we shall necessarily be discussing information about the performance and disposition of clinical resources.

It is often argued that information is power but the authors would argue that this is simplistic; information is power only if the owner understands what it means and knows how to use it. It may be useful here to discuss the distinction between data, information, knowledge, and wisdom, which lie on a spectrum as shown in Figure 8.1:

- data: a collection of numbers, letters, sounds, and pictures
- information: data structured into meaningful sets relevant to a particular situation
- knowledge: information combined with an understanding of what it means and how to use it
- wisdom: knowledge combined with an understanding of when to use it and what the implications will be.

When you make a decision, it is important to be able to have access to the information you need; however, you will have views about the quality of the information you need. If information is to be of value to you it must satisfy some important criteria, as shown in Box 8.1.

| Data | Information | Knowledge | Wisdom |

Figure 8.1: The information spectrum.

Box 8.1: Information for decision making

Criterion	Explanation
Timing	The information must be available when you need it
Presentation	The information must be presented to you in a form which you can easily understand and use
Accuracy	The information must be accurate enough for you to be able to rely on it
Relevance	It must be possible to understand the significance of the information to the topic under discussion

---

Data, and hence the information derived from it, comes from two different classes of source, primary and secondary, and may be quantitative, obtained by counting things, or qualitative, obtained by soliciting people's opinions (Table 8.1). You will also be aware of information which appears to be a kind of hybrid of quantitative and qualitative information, which results from asking a number of people to record the extent to which they like or agree with subjective statements. This approach is common in quality audits, using an approach such as that illustrated in Figure 8.2; this is sometimes referred to as a Likert scale. The results of such a question are numerical; taken on their own they are of little value but, if you ask the same question again in a year's time and the number of people responding 'very good' or 'good' has increased, this is a reliable indication that things are improving.

Research into the information needs of people at different levels in organizations reveals that, as managers move up the management hierarchy, they make less use of internal information, over whose quality they have some control, and more use of external information over which they have little or no control, as shown in Figure 8.3.[1] Furthermore, this external information comes from a bewildering array of sources, is almost all secondary, is of dubious validity, and unknown reliability. Hence the need for senior managers to make decisions which are based on a combination of experience, data, and hunch.

Table 8.1: Examples of classes of information

	Primary	Secondary
Quantitative	Number of patients seen at your outpatients clinic	National waiting list statistics
Qualitative	Patients' opinions about the quality of the food provided by your Trust	Patients' opinions about the quality of the food provided by large acute Trusts across the UK

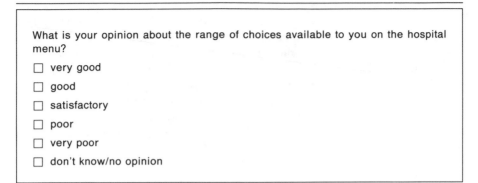

What is your opinion about the range of choices available to you on the hospital menu?

☐ very good

☐ good

☐ satisfactory

☐ poor

☐ very poor

☐ don't know/no opinion

Figure 8.2: Subjective question in questionnaire.

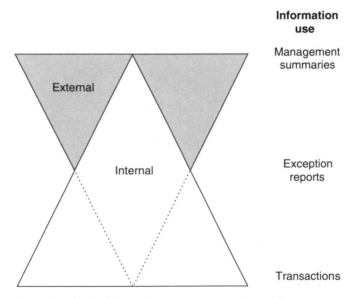

Figure 8.3: Use of information in the management hierarchy.

As a clinical director you will be interested primarily in management information, which is information about physical resources and money, such as:

• budgets

• bed vacancies

• contracts

• costs

• training.

However some of the data from which this information is derived, such as that about the numbers of investigations carried out, or patients discharged, is collected as the result of clinical activity. This is resource management information, which is the intersection between clinical and management information (Figure 8.4). This has an important impact on the design of information technology (IT) systems because, in order to eliminate the duplication of effort in data entry and the concomitant risk of error, it is important to position both clinical and management information systems within the same overall framework.

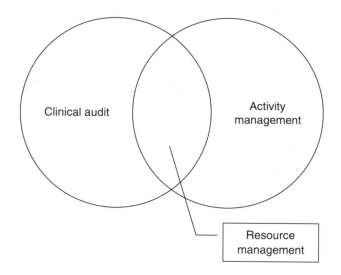

Figure 8.4: Relationship between clinical and management information.

Information systems in the NHS are subject to the strategic trends which are transforming the use of IT throughout the world; in many cases Trusts are jumping straight from 1970s systems and technology into the 1990s, where the expectations are for increases in:

- networking
- sharing of information within and between departments
- importance of corporate standards for operating systems
- use of electronic communications

and for the involvement of almost everyone in the use of information systems.

Networking

So why is there all this emphasis on networking? There are many reasons but one of the most important is that networks give users the opportunity of sharing data quickly and accurately. However, if the volumes and frequency of data sharing are small, handing a floppy disk to your colleague is a viable method of data sharing. The means commonly used in the past although fortunately not so much in the 1990s was that data would be printed by one system and then entered onto another system through the keyboard, with all the attendant risks of transcription errors, differences of interpretation, and wasted time (Figure 8.5). However, with the large volumes of clinical and management data which are of interest to many people across a Trust, the arguments in favour of some form of electronic networking are irresistible.

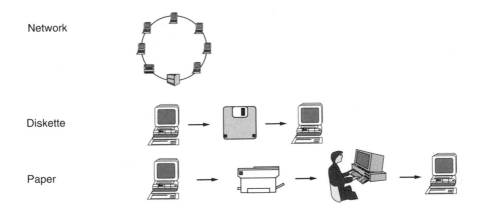

Figure 8.5: Ways of transferring data.

In recent years there have been two fundamentally different responses to the requirement for networks: centralized systems, such as that described by the Hospital Information Systems Strategy (HISS) and distributed systems such as Case Mix Management Systems (CMMS). Centralized systems start with the assumption that the best way of providing the wide range of systems required by clinicians and managers is to develop and implement a complete new system which suffers from none of the handicaps, such as old equipment and out-of-date systems design, common to existing hospital systems. Centralized systems are therefore complex, large-scale, and costly, and although a number of hospitals have adopted this approach there are, as yet, few successful, fully implemented systems. Distributed systems start from the opposite assumption that, because of the complexity of hospitals and the continually changing requirements, the best solution is to provide a framework within which existing systems and new systems can operate, sharing information where appropriate but allowing directorates and departments to maintain their own private information about activities, such as research, which are of no relevance to other directorates and departments. Distributed systems can be implemented gradually and directorates and departments can change or replace their own systems as long as they conform to the rules governing the interchange of common data. An important function of both centralized and distributed systems is to act as a repository for financial and resource information, which is the basis for management decision making at both Trust and directorate level (Table 8.2).

Table 8.2: Centralized and distributed systems

Characteristic	Centralized	Distributed
Objective	Total management of hospital	Resource planning
Architecture	Mainframe with terminals	Networked work group systems
Cost	Large capital investment	Incremental
Current systems	Replaced	Integrated into CMMS
Clinical data	Centralized	Dispersed
Management data	Centralized	Centralized
Security	Complex access control procedures	Only 'hospital data' is shared; other data is held at work group level
Design of directorate systems	Dictated from centre	At discretion of directorate
Implementation	Big bang, can be disruptive	Incremental, can be phased across directorates
Ownership of data	Trust	Shared between Trust and directorates

You may prefer the distributed model, particularly if you are engaged in any form of research where your research data is held in systems which are an extension of your current clinical management systems.

In many hospitals, the Patient Administration System (PAS) has been the backbone of hospital information systems for up to 20 years. However, PAS is an out-of-date systems concept usually running on obsolete technology and, whether centralized or distributed systems are the chosen route, the PAS is usually one of the first systems to be replaced. In distributed systems (Figure 8.6) it is usually replaced by a system called the Master Patient Index, or something similar, which is an index which enables all directorates and departments to index their clinical activity data in a consistent way, together with parts of other systems which handle such activities as admissions and outpatients appointments.

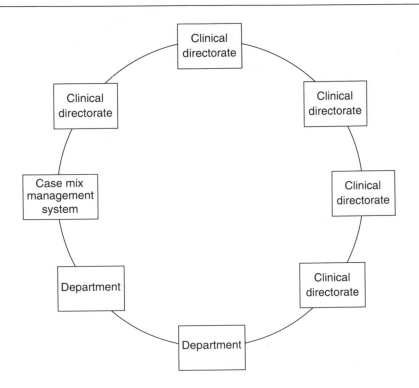

Figure 8.6: Typical distributed system.

In the distributed model, where each directorate and department has its own local system, the commonest model for recently installed and new systems is the Local Area Network (LAN) as shown in Figure 8.7. This system contains all the resources – personal computers, printers, and file server (large local disk storage) – to satisfy the needs of a work group such as a directorate management team and its secretaries, without recourse to central resources.

Information strategy

Information technology now constitutes one of the biggest areas of investment for most Trusts, and it is therefore necessary to develop an information technology strategy to guide the development of IT systems over a period of some years. Table 8.3 gives some useful guidelines for developing an information strategy although some of them, such as those referring to a telecommunication policy and an IT director, apply to Trusts rather than to clinical directorates.[2]

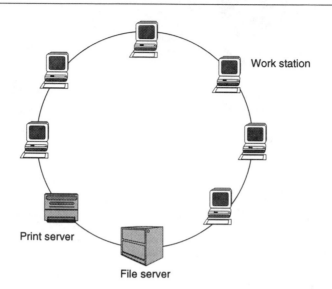

Figure 8.7: Typical Local Area Network.

Table 8.3: Information strategy questions

Activity	Recurring questions	New questions
Planning	What systems should we develop next? Which of our many application needs has priority? What is the next hardware step?	What information systems do our current business strategies demand? What strategic opportunities are presented by information technology? Do we need a telecommunication policy?
Organization	Should computing be centralized or distributed? How do we improve relations between users and systems specialists? How can we secure support from top management?	How will information technology affect our organization's structure? How can we find more IT staff? Should we have an IT Director?
Control	How much should we spend on IT? Are we getting value for money from IT? Should we charge out all our IT services?	How much are we spending on IT? How can we evaluate IT? How can we manage a large IT project?

This task necessarily falls on the IT department but it is in your interest to ensure that they have a proper understanding of your requirements. The best way of doing this is to state them in terms of the timing, content, and presentation of the information you need to manage; you may also want to gain access to subsets of your data so that you can manipulate them in ways which you find helpful. The IT professionals will then question you to discover what and where the source data is and to gain an understanding of what has to be done to it to provide you with the information you need. However, there are several different approaches to the management of the IT resource, as illustrated in Table 8.4.[3]

Table 8.4: Types of management control of IT

Equipment configuration	Centralized	Decentralized
Centralized	All analysts, programmers, operations staff at central site	Analysts and programmers work for various departments, making use of a central resource through terminals
Distributed	All analysts and programmers controlled by central site but assigned to different departments; programs down-loaded to distributed processors	All program development done departmentally; control through standards and procedures; central coordinating group optional
Decentralized	Analysts and programmers assigned to departments	Complete local control over systems and operations staff

Your information requirements are unique, and you may feel that the only way in which they can be met is by developing a system specifically to meet your requirements. However, there are now many different clinical departmental information systems packages on the market, many of them with a substantial installed population. In IT systems, as with many other aspects of management, it is often necessary to accept that a 90 per cent solution is affordable and that the cost of the remaining 10 per cent is greater than can be justified by the additional benefits it provides. Sometimes, a low-tech solution will work as well as a high-tech one; in one hospital where the authors were working the most cost effective way of getting urgent pathology and radiology requests and reports around the hospital was to install fax machines in departments and wards, at a cost of a few hundred pounds a machine and no investment in computer technology. However, there are now several standard packaged application systems on the market offering word processing, spreadsheets, presentation aids, and databases, each with a large measure of sophistication and a variety of tools to support the inexperienced user. You may well find that you or one of your colleagues has the aptitude and interest to be able to develop some interim solutions.

Data entry and validation

Since the beginning of the computer revolution in the 1950s much thought has been given to the task of ensuring that the data entered into a computer system is valid and meaningful. We are all used to the common forms of data validation used in packaged program systems – examples are the spell checker and grammar checker in a word processor and the date and currency validation checkers in spreadsheets – but for some Trust systems the requirements are less straightforward. For instance, it is easy to check that a clerk enters a valid hospital number, but less easy to check that the number entered corresponds with the patient to whom it is supposed to refer. And it is easy to check that a valid diagnostic or procedure code (HRG, Read, OPCS-4, ICD-10) has been entered but less easy to check that the code relates to the actual diagnosis or procedure for that patient. In each case, the only person who can realistically validate the data is the clinician who created it – the nurse knows that F262272 is the Mrs Smith on Ward B2 and the surgeon knows that he operated on her varicose veins, not her gall bladder. As computer systems become increasingly user-friendly and even more widespread the arguments in favour of clinicians doing their own clinical coding and entering their own data will become even more powerful (Table 8.5). And, as IT professionals have long said 'garbage in, garbage out' – management and clinical information are of little or no value if they are based on invalid data.

Table 8.5: Data entry: the pros and cons

	You do it	**Coding clerk does it**
Timing	When it happens	When she gets to the paperwork in her in-tray
Coding	You know what the condition is	She has to work it out from your notes – and sometimes gets it wrong
Keying error	If you make one you notice because the data is meaningful	She may not notice
Effort	No more than writing it down	Waste of effort – you write it down and she transcribes it

Data security

Data security is a portmanteau word for two important features of information systems management: protection of data against loss and protection of data against unauthorized access.

Preventing loss of data is a simple but often overlooked process – it requires two things only:

- saving files regularly when you are working on them to ensure that the work you have done during the past two hours is not going to be lost because of a power cut; most systems provide a facility for the file to be saved automatically at specified intervals – every ten minutes is a good compromise between losing nothing and being continually held up by the file saving activity

- backing up all the files on a computer at regular intervals – say every week – and the files that have been created or changed at intervening periods – say every day. Since the IT department will be backing up all centrally held files, the only ones you need to back up are those which you hold on your own PC or are held on the file server on your LAN. There is a variety of different systems for backing up files – the best, in terms of speed and capacity, are those which use tape cartridges or re-writeable optical disks. Your IT department should be able to advise which is the best for you.

Protection of data against unauthorized access is a theoretically complex subject but fortunately simple to implement at a personal level. Most PC operating systems, such as Windows, have built in password facilities to restrict access to the PC, and individual software systems have passwords to restrict access to files created by those systems. The rules for passwords are:

- as soon as you gain access to a new system, change the initial password

- do not use a word which someone else is likely to be able to guess, like the name of the directorate or a member of your family

- change your password(s) at regular intervals

- do not write them down in a place or in such a way as to enable anyone to guess where they are or what they are.

An acquaintance of one of the authors has hit on the idea of choosing his passwords from a wine guide although he has to abbreviate them because, as he remarked, not many chateau names consist of eight or less letters.

The main argument of this chapter is to emphasize the need for clinical directors and others to take responsibility for the definition, collection, and use of the data and information they use. IT professionals can provide the infrastructure and can acquire or develop systems to meet your needs – but if your needs are not clearly thought through and articulated the IT professionals are unlikely to be able to guess them.

References

1 Austin N. (1986) *A management support environment.* ICL Technical Journal. OUP.
2 Earl M. (1989) *Management strategies for information technology.* Prentice Hall.
3 Lucas H. (1992) *Information systems: concepts for management.* McGraw Hill.

Quality

Noel Austin

Management is responsible for 94 per cent of quality problems and their first step should be to dismantle the barriers that prevent employees doing a good job.

Deming, 1986[1]

In some ways, the authors could argue that this final chapter on quality is superfluous, since all the topics covered in earlier chapters are designed to improve the quality of clinical directorate management and hence of delivered care. The main counter-argument is that in the NHS, as in the public and private sectors in most developed countries, a quality 'industry' has developed which focuses more or less exclusively on the quality of every aspect of a Trust's behaviour and outputs. Indeed,

> Quality is needed at every link, otherwise the chain will be broken, and the failure will usually find its way sooner or later to the interface between the organization and the patient. It is those who work at that interface who experience the problems of records or x-rays not being available, or transport not arriving, or the lack of clean laundry, or shabby furniture which adversely affects the service given to the patients, but the failure has occurred some time previously at some other point in the chain.[2]

The quality 'industry' can claim the credit for bringing about a significant change in the attitudes of people in public and private sectors across the UK – the recognition that everyone with whom you deal, whether a patient, a GP, a health authority, or commission (external), or any member of your directorate's or your Trust's management and staff (internal), is a customer. As Morris implies, each member of this chain of people throughout the organization must provide a quality service if the ultimate customer – the patient – is to receive quality care. This is reflected in the attitudes of HM Government, of the Royal Colleges, and of the other clinical professional bodies.

But can we justify the claim that recommendations contained in earlier chapters of this book have an impact on delivered quality? Box 9.1 attempts to do so.

Box 9.1: Quality impact of aspects of management

Chapter	Contribution to quality
Chapter 1: Working in teams	Improving relations with other team members Improving relations with other teams Improving the team's efficiency and effectiveness
Chapter 2: Managing people	Recruiting good people Keeping staff up-to-date with training Motivating staff Maintaining performance levels
Chapter 3: Negotiating	Achieving results which minimize aggravation Making the best overall use of scarce resources
Chapter 4: Managing change	Minimizing disruption Improving service delivery Introducing new services and processes
Chapter 5: Strategic planning	Making the most effective use of directorate resources Developing and financing new services Exploiting favourable environmental changes Ameliorating the effects of adverse environmental changes
Chapter 6: Service delivery planning	Front line service quality Service Level Agreements Detailed resource planning Monitoring service delivery performance
Chapter 7: Managing financially	Making the most efficient use of financial resources Releasing financial resources for service improvements
Chapter 8: Information	Monitoring service delivery performance Improving communication within the directorate and Trust

So what is quality? It has variously been defined as 'conformance to requirements';[3] 'the degree of conformance of all the relevant features and characteristics of the product (or service) to all aspects of a customer's need, limited by the price and delivery he or she will accept';[4] 'the totality of features and characteristics of a product or service that bear on its ability to satisfy stated or implied needs';[5] and 'fitness for purpose'.[6] There is an important distinction, alluded to in Groocock's definition, between quality and excellence which is particularly relevant to the NHS; while excellence is about delivering the absolute best based on criteria set by the service deliverer, quality is about achieving the best that can be delivered within the resources made available by HM Government. Few people would challenge the assertion that Concorde demonstrates engineering excellence but the consortium's failure to sell more than half a dozen planes vividly illustrates that it did not enable service providers to deliver a service at prices that travellers were prepared to pay.

Total Quality Management

Total Quality Management (TQM) is an approach to quality which is at best a way of life and at worst a meaningless buzzword.

> TQM is a cost-effective approach, involving everyone in the organization, continually to improve the quality of service provided in order to satisfy the customer.

An approach to TQM is set out in Box 9.2.[7]

In summary, what all these various texts are saying is that everyone must be conscious of delivering quality all the time; in a Trust context this includes all clinical and support staff in every directorate and department, finance, general management, estates, catering, housekeeping, and portering. To bring about such a radical change in philosophy is evidently a major task and perhaps the most common source of disappointment in implementing TQM in an organization, whether in the NHS or elsewhere, is the failure to recognize the scope of the project.

A more tightly focused view of quality is that which you mean when you include quality standards in contracts and service agreements. Several approaches have been developed, all of which bring insights into what we mean by quality in service delivery and how it can be achieved. Berry et al.[8] developed a list of criteria for service quality which is shown in Table 9.1 together with examples of how these criteria may be fulfilled or not; you will spot several NHS parallels. The great strength of this list is that, although based on research into a wide variety of industries in the USA, it contains aspects of service provision that are easy to recognize and do something about.

Box 9.2: How to achieve TQM

Focus clearly on the needs of your customers, internal and external.

Achieve a top-quality performance in all areas.

Operate the simple procedures necessary for the achievement of a quality performance.

Critically and continually examine all processes to remove non-productive activities and waste.

See the improvements required and develop measures of performance.

Develop the team approach to problem solving.

Develop good procedures for communication and acknowledgement of good work.

Review continually the processes to develop the strategy of never-ending improvement.

Table 9.1: Customer assessment of quality

Factors	Good examples	Bad examples
Reliability	Punctual arrival of train	Failure to 'phone customer back as agreed
Responsiveness	Maintenance staff who service equipment at short notice	Long queues
Competence	Staff carry out task with skill and competence	Bank fails to cancel standing order and then charges fee for resulting overdraft
Access	Easy to find one's way Easy to get to	Poor signing Limited car parking
Courtesy	Polite and helpful staff	Senior staff patronizing and condescending
Communication	Medical staff who explain the diagnosis and alternative forms of treatment without jargon	Lack of information when trains are delayed as to the cause and duration of the delay
Credibility	A solicitor you feel you can trust and depend on	A used-car salesman who tries hard-sell tactics
Security	A feeling of personal safety and confidentiality	Unlit access at night
Understanding/ knowing the customer	Staff who make an effort to meet a customer's individual requirements	Staff who don't recognize a regular customer
Tangibles	Pleasing physical appearance of facilities and staff	Poor, out-of-date equipment being used for the service

In the NHS, Sir Robert Maxwell, Secretary of the King's Fund Foundation, suggested some specific dimensions of health care quality, shown with examples in Box 9.3.[9]

Box 9.3: Dimensions of quality

Dimension	Examples
Access to services	Are services convenient geographically? Are waiting times for treatment, the physical design of buildings, the availability of transport and car parking acceptable?
Equity	Are services provided to all types of patients whatever their cultural, racial, or social background?
Relevance to need	Do services reflect well the needs of the population served? Are there any gaps?
Social acceptability	Is the way services are provided acceptable to the people they are intended to serve?
Efficiency	Are services delivered as efficiently as possible within the resources available? Are they cost effective and appropriately staffed?
Effectiveness	Do services achieve the intended benefits and outcomes in terms of the health of the people served?

Another relevant and important set of criteria for the delivery of quality service come from *Working for patients* (Box 9.4).[10]

Making quality happen

There is evidently no shortage of advice about what constitutes quality, and yet the authors have seen quality programmes in NHS Trusts experience considerable difficulties, or even grind to a halt, as a result of the failure of participants to recognize that quality was everyone's responsibility and that different professional paradigms inevitably gave participants different views of what constituted quality. The quality gurus (Crosby,[3] Deming,[1] Juran,[6] and Oakland[11]) take broadly similar approaches to implementing quality, summarized in Box 9.5, which again contains echoes of many of the topics covered in earlier chapters.

Box 9.4: Quality guidelines

The appropriateness of treatment and care.

Achievement of optimum clinical outcome.

All clinically-recognized procedures to minimize complications and similar preventable events.

An attitude which treats patients with dignity and as individuals.

An environment conducive to patient safety, reassurance, and contentment.

Speed of response to patient needs and minimum inconvenience to them (and their relatives and friends).

The involvement of patients in their own care.

Box 9.5: Making quality happen

Commitment and example from top management: senior managers must not treat quality as 'flavour of the month', to be put on one side when something more urgent arises.

Commitment across the organization: everyone has a responsibility to improve the quality of what he does; the physician, the nurse, and the porter all have an impact on the quality of a patient's life in hospital.

Customer focus: improvements in efficiency may help you to address budgetary problems but are futile if they do not lead to an improvement in customer satisfaction.

Participation and teamwork: it is difficult to get staff to take part in quality initiatives but in the NHS the great majority of staff are committed to care; the task is therefore to help them to realize that improvements in quality are the same as, or will lead to, improvements in care.

Continuous improvement: quality is a moving target, partly because few people can ever claim that they deliver 100% quality and partly because customer expectations change, being influenced by past experience, by the comments of friends and relatives, and by the media to expect ever increasing quality of care.

Supplier quality: as was indicated in Chapter 6, you cannot deliver quality service to your customers unless you receive quality service from your suppliers; managing the supplier relationship is therefore a key aspect of managing quality.

BS 5750 and ISO 9000

Both the British Standards Institution and the International Standards Organization have defined standards setting out what an organization has to do to demonstrate that it is delivering a quality service to its customers; BS 5750 is rapidly being supplanted by ISO 9000 and its variants (ISO 9001 and ISO 9002) with which it is almost identical. For an organization which is already providing a quality service, which means that it knows what is meant by quality in its industry, has specified how services will be delivered at that quality, and monitors that service delivery meets the specifications (Figure 9.1[12]), achieving accreditation to ISO 9000 is a straightforward process. Organizations which are not systematic in their approach to service delivery find the process a bureaucratic nightmare. Nevertheless, governmental and other organizations are

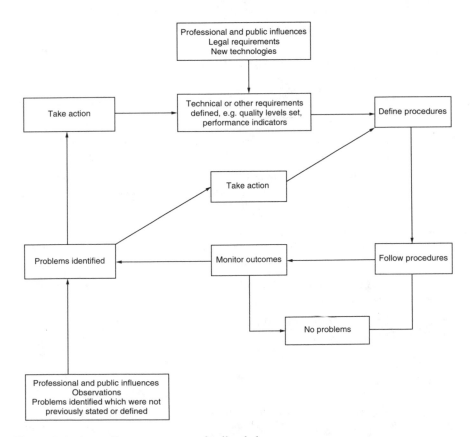

Figure 9.1: A quality system as a feedback loop.

increasingly making ISO 9000 accreditation a condition of awarding contracts. The benefits of ISO 9000 implementation are that it:

- makes you state your objectives in providing a service
- causes you to set up systems to define services and keep records of how they are delivered
- requires you to audit the process of service delivery
- necessitates a clear definition of who is responsible for what
- leads to auditable systems which can be verified by external agencies.

However, although you may be required to take part in the process of acquiring accreditation it is likely that this will be driven at a Trust level, although there are examples of departments such as radiology, theatres, and catering seeking accreditation at a departmental level.

The key lesson of this chapter is that quality is not just a fad, to be discarded in favour of the next fashion that comes along. Quality is about:

- ensuring that the whole team is aligned to the achievement of the directorate's objectives and that they work effectively together to achieve those objectives
- ensuring that every member of the directorate is trained, motivated, and managed in such a way as to enable them to maximize their contribution to the achievement of those objectives
- negotiating contracts and service level agreements which optimize the use of the directorate's resources and those of its suppliers and customers
- creating in the directorate an attitude which enables it to respond to new and changing customer requirements, whether those changes are required by external or internal customers
- continually monitoring changes in the external environment and in customers' likely requirements in such a way that your strategic plans maximize your ability to be able to meet future customer needs
- defining, delivering, monitoring, and refining service delivery to meet patient needs and expectations
- using financial and other planning and monitoring information to make the best use of your resources.

References

1 Deming W. (1986) *Out of the crisis*. Massachusetts Institute of Technology.
2 Morris B. (1989) Totaly quality management. *International Journal of Health Care Quality Assurance*.

3 Crosby P. (1984) *Quality without tears.* McGraw Hill.
4 Groocock J. (1986) *The chain of quality.* Wiley.
5 International Standards Organization (1986) Quality vocabulary. Part I International terms. ISO.
6 Juran J. (1986) The quality trilogy. In: *Quality progress* **19**(8): 19–24.
7 Department of Trade and Industry. (1990) *Total quality management: a practical approach.* DTI.
8 Berry L, Zeitaml V and Parasuraman A. (1985) *A practical approach to quality.* Joiner Associates.
9 Maxwell R. (1984) Quality assessment in health. *BMJ.* **288**: 1470–2.
10 Working for patients (1989). HMSO.
11 Oakland J. (1989) *Total quality management.* Heinemann.
12 Rooney M. (1994) Applying common sense. In: *B701 Managing health service delivery resource book.* Open University.

Index